The Way o

Dreams & Visions

Third Edition

COLETTE TOACH

Interpreting Your Secret
Conversations with God

AMI BOOKSHOP

www.ami-bookshop.com

The Way of Dreams and Visions

Third Edition

ISBN-10: 1626640025
ISBN-13: 978-1-62664-002-3

1st **Printing** September 2000 – ISBN # 978-0971985919
2nd **Edition** November 2013
3rd **Edition** April 2016

Published by **Apostolic Movement International, LLC**
E-mail Address: admin@ami-bookshop.com
Web Address: www.ami-bookshop.com

Dedication

I would like to dedicate this book to my best friend, problem solver, life changer, tear wiper and groom... Jesus Christ.

Lord I love you more than life and without you I could never have prepared the words on these pages. I dedicate this book to you in its entirety. May you take it and use it to bless every person who picks it up to glean the truths from it. I give you the license and rights to this book and as I hand it to you, may you put your seal of approval on it.

I do not profess that these words have come out of my own human understanding, but give you all the glory, my friend and my daddy - the ever loving and ever real Lord Jesus Christ!

Contents

Dream Interpretation By the Spirit

These things we also speak, not in words which man's wisdom teaches but which the Holy Spirit teaches, comparing spiritual things with spiritual.

~ 1 Corinthians 2:13

Chapter 01 – Dream Interpretation by the Spirit

Everyone Dreams

Dream interpretation has become a big thing these days. People have this idea in their minds that if you can interpret dreams, it is like you have something special. You are able to see into somebody's life; you are able to see into their future, and it has pretty much been put on par with being a psychic. If you can interpret dreams, you must be something phenomenal. And even in the world today you will find books on dream interpretation. You will find books on symbols in dreams, so that you can piece together an interpretation of your dream, and somehow in that interpretation, find direction, guidance and perhaps answers to the problems you face in life.

I would like to approach dream interpretation in perhaps a way that it has not been approached before. I want to begin by saying that interpreting dreams is not something that a psychic does. Interpreting dreams is not something to give you knowledge of the future and to give you hidden secrets and meanings to things that are not obvious.

When it comes to the Christian life and our Christian walk, dreams are very simply put, as stated in Scripture: night visions. Dreams, given by the Spirit of God, are no different to prophecy. They are no different to visions.

They are no different to a word of knowledge or a word of wisdom given by the Spirit of the Lord in the congregation. Dreams are simply another way that the Lord would choose to speak to you, His servant, at His given time.

I want to expand on the subject, but the foundational point that I want you to understand before we begin, is that dreams are simply a way of your spirit and the Holy Spirit, giving you the messages that He would like to give you. It could be in a vision during the day or in prayer, or a vision at night on your bed. It is the same thing. Dreams are not something supernatural. It is not something fantastic that only the special and elect have. It is a function of the human spirit that in fact, every single human has. A dream is simply your spirit communicating to your mind, all the stimuli you have been pushing into it that day.

This is not something that just believers have. Even unbelievers have dreams. But the difference between a believer and an unbeliever is that the believer has within them the indwelling of the Holy Spirit. This is where the division comes. A believer is able to have prophetic dreams.

Now, some of what I am going to teach on here can apply to both believers and unbelievers, but you will find parallels. But where the line is drawn is that the believer can have a prophetic dream, but an unbeliever cannot, because they do not have the indwelling of the Holy Spirit and they are not capable of hearing from their spirits, because the Scripture says they are dead. They are not able to receive knowledge and wisdom from the Spirit of God, for their spirits are dead to the realm of God.

This is where the line is drawn. I know that there has been a lot of confusion, and a lot of Christians have gone astray by getting into things that they should not have been, by looking to the worldly books and looking for worldly answers and symbolism. You need to realize that as a Christian, your spirit has been recreated in Christ. It now has the ability to commune with God and to receive His information, His thoughts for you, His feelings for you, and His vision for you – by dreams, visions, prophecy, word of knowledge or word of wisdom.

Who Can Have a Prophetic Dream?

I would like to begin by asking, "Who can have a prophetic dream?" I think I have covered this pretty well, but let's look at 1 Corinthians 12:11...

> *"But one and the same Spirit works all these things, distributing to each one individually as He wills."*

For All Christians

In 1 Corinthians 12, Paul is talking about the gifts of the Spirit. Everybody, every Christian, is capable of having a prophetic dream. Why? Because they have the indwelling of the Holy Spirit, and just as we come together in a meeting and every member is given a word of knowledge or a vision or something to share from the Spirit of God, so too does every Christian have the ability to have a prophetic dream. This is not solely for the prophet, as many people may think. Even though the prophet does function in a lot of the revelatory gifts, more so than the average believer, that is not to say that every believer cannot operate in those ministry gifts, because it is the Holy Spirit who imparts those gifts and manifests those gifts as He wills.

Being a Christian entitles you to those gifts just as much as if you were standing in one of the Ministry Offices. So do not think that because you are not a prophet and you do not perhaps flow in as many gifts as the prophet does, that you are not able to have prophetic dreams or visions, or that you are not able to interpret your dreams. This is not like the Old Testament, where only the prophets received revelation from their dreams.

But you see, in the Old Testament, they did not have the indwelling of the Holy Spirit. So what would happen is that the Holy Spirit would move spontaneously on an individual, and impart to them the knowledge of the Spirit for a particular moment; for a particular time. And that particular time depended on their righteousness before God.

But we do not stand in that position anymore since Christ has come. Now we maintain the Spirit within us. And we, at any given time, can tap into the wisdom that is within our own spirits. This is what I really want to encourage you to reach out and receive from the Lord right now. To receive that wisdom and the gifts to be able to discern and receive revelation from the Holy Spirit for yourself, not just in dream interpretation, but also in visions and every other sense the Lord may try to use to speak to you. This is something for you as an individual, as a servant of the Lord. This is your inheritance from the Lord Jesus Christ.

Who Can Interpret Dreams?

The only prerequisite for dream interpretation and flowing in the gifts is desire. Consider this passage in 1 Corinthians 14:1…

> *"Pursue love, and desire spiritual gifts, but especially that you may prophesy."*

There is only one condition, one prerequisite for you being able to flow in the gifts, and that is that you earnestly desire them. "If we then, being evil, know how to give good gifts to our children, how much more will our Father in heaven give good gifts to those that ask Him." If you would just desire those gifts for yourself and earnestly, passionately cry out to the Lord, there is nothing that He will withhold from you, His child. If even we, as humans, can give our children those things they desire, your Heavenly Father desires to give you those things that would meet the desire of your heart.

If you have really been crying out to Him to hear His voice, to receive His revelation, to understand those things He is trying to speak to you; if you would reach out by faith and earnestly desire, there is nothing that the Lord will withhold from you, His servant.

4 Categories of Dreams

I would like to look at the four different categories of dreams. The first three can apply to unbelievers as well as believers. That is your healing dream, a purging dream, and a garbage dream. Those three can apply to believers and unbelievers. But the fourth applies to believers only. That is the prophetic dream. That is where the Holy Spirit moves upon you and gives you a message from within.

1st Category - The Healing Dream

The first type of dream, the healing dream, takes place when there comes a shift and a change in your templates. We have covered templates in other teachings, so I am just going to skim through it very quickly. Templates are formed in your life through circumstances that you have faced. As you have faced events; as you have faced hurts; as you have faced things in your life, you have built up a reaction to those circumstances. And as you pass through life, as you are faced with the same situation, you will find the exact same reaction coming out of you. You will be angry at the same set of circumstances. You will rejoice when the same set of circumstances occurs. You will find yourself acting repeatedly in the same way to the same set of circumstances. They are templates formed in us from the day of our birth.

We all know, "Put your hand in the hot plate, and it is going to burn."

That is a template. You know, "If I put my hand in the fire, it is going to burn." Why? How did you learn that? As a child you put your finger in the flame, or you thought you would play with matches, and you were hurt. A template was formed. Fire equals pain. So every time you are faced with fire what happens? Fear grips you, because you remember, "I put my hand in the fire as a child and it burnt. Fear!" So every time you are faced with fire, that same fear will come up. That is just an example of what a template is.

You may face circumstances in your daily life that will change that template. You will face a circumstance that brings a shift in that template in a Christian context. You may come into a situation where the Lord brings up a painful memory from the past, as in say, being burnt by fire. Perhaps you had a bad experience as a child and you developed a tremendous fear. The Lord will move in and bring healing to that template, so that when you are faced with that circumstance again the fear is there no longer.

Now this is what a healing dream accomplishes. After the Lord has ministered healing to that memory, you will go to sleep that night and there will come a shift. Perhaps you will relive the original memory where you were hurt. Perhaps you will dream that as an adult you are facing that memory, but this time you are in control. It can vary. But the point is, as you wake up you feel victorious having faced that event again in your life, but this time not being gripped by that fear; this time you are not failing.

Perhaps you were somebody who was rejected as a child and adolescent. Perhaps you were a teenager that could never fit in with the students around you, and you were always the little guy sitting in the corner. And so as a result you built up walls around yourself to hide your insecurity. Then the Lord brings you through a time of death, of pulling those walls aside and pouring in love and healing, and He lifts up that little rejected child to stand. That evening you may have a dream where you are facing your peers. But this time you are not feeling insecure anymore. This time they are praising you and telling you how wonderful you are.

Perhaps you were picked on by a teacher as a child, but in your dream this teacher is praising you and saying that you are wonderful. Or perhaps you are standing up to the teacher and saying, "Hey, stop doing that to me! It is wrong." And you wake up feeling that you have accomplished and had a victory.

A healing dream is simply an indication that something has changed within you; that you have experienced some kind of healing. So you identify a healing dream by dreaming of past fears or events, but waking up victorious having faced your fears. It shows that the Lord has been at work in you; that your templates have been shifted and changed to accommodate the new you.

2nd Category - The Cleansing or Purging Dream

The next dream is the cleansing dream. These dreams are by far the most common. As you walk through your day you face temptations, you face fights, strife and pressure. You face all kinds of stimuli that are coming at you from all sides. Your boss got on your case, your husband is giving you a tough time, the kids have been screaming. You have built up these emotions within, and you have tried to remain in control during the day. The chances are that night you are dreaming you are bashing your boss in the nose. You have built up all that anger during the day and you have controlled yourself, but in your dreams you may actually dream that you are doing exactly as you desired to do during the day, but held back on.

These are cleansing dreams, and all they do is simply let your inner man express the temptations and desires and all the natural, fleshly passions out in your dream in a safe environment where you are not affecting anybody or hurting anybody, and it gives you a release. It gives you a relief. As you dream these cleansing dreams, all that built up and pent up emotion that sits in your stomach, is released. And when you wake up you feel relieved of that pressure and that anger that was built in you from the night before.

This is what happens during your REM sleep. And if you do not have these dreams, you could have a nervous breakdown, because you need to release them. You need that emotional release in your dreams, and it is a

God-given natural gift given to the human mind to give release of those emotions and stress. Because if you did not get to release all that was inside, it would build up to such a degree that it would give you a nervous breakdown.

I know that psychologists have taken this and they have gone to the extreme. They have said, "Well, if you have got built-up anger and if you have built-up bitterness, you need to act out on it," and they give you a pillow to beat up and bash.

"Pretend this is your mother-in-law and give it a good beating."

But the Lord has given man a natural means to get rid of the pent up emotion, grief and pain that is within them, and it can be found in their dreams. This is one of the most popular and most common expressions of dream that you will have, and probably have every single evening, even if you cannot remember your dreams. If you remember dreaming a lot but you wake up and you cannot remember your dreams, it is very likely that those dreams were cleansing and simply purged all the emotion, struggle and temptations that you faced during that day. So those dreams, where you find yourself living out emotions and desires that you would never do in real life, are very likely cleansing dreams.

3rd Category - The Garbage Dream

The third type of dream is the garbage dream. You wake up and remember it, but really it is just garbage. It is about nothing in particular. It is just simply your inner man throwing out junk.

This happens particularly when you get into the Word or start filling yourself with teaching. You start feeding your mind with those things of Christ to start adapting your mind to become the mind of Christ. What happens, is all the stimuli you have been feeding in by reading books, watching movies and getting involved in bad conversations – all those negative stimuli that you have been feeding in get rattled a little in there. Now you are starting to feed in the light and the life of the Word. And as you start doing that your mind is going to start throwing out the junk and the garbage that you have been feeding in there for years.

You could have dreams about movies you saw when you were a child. Do you know how much garbage you have accumulated in your mind since you were a child? How many movies you watched? How many books you have read? How much radio you have listened to? How much, not so good conversations that you have gotten involved with? You know how much negative stimuli you fill your mind with all around you every day?

Now as you get into the Word and start pouring the water in, it is going to start pushing the junk out. I often use a lovely description of dropping a stone into a beautiful clear lake. It looks beautiful and clear until you drop that stone in, and all the rubbish in the bottom of the lake begins to get stirred up. And before you know it the water starts to become murky.

That is what happens when you start applying the Word and you start refreshing your mind of all the garbage that has been in there all along. It starts coming out. This applies very much to the unbeliever as well. As they feed more garbage in, they are going to be getting more garbage out as well. As they feed in more movies and books and everything that is of the world, the strife and contamination and fear, that is what is going to be reflected in their dreams as well. They are pushing in garbage, and garbage is coming out, and there is just a continual flow of garbage in and out. There is not a cleansing coming.

Garbage dreams are identified by many scene changes with many confused events and emotions. There is no single purpose in the dream and you find yourself being shifted from one event to the next. Every event seems to flow into the next and you wake up with many different impressions, pictures and emotions.

If you are facing this right now, continue with the Word. Remove yourself from anything that would contaminate you, that is not of the Spirit of God, and continue feeding yourself with the Word. As you do this, there is going to start coming a clarity in your dreams. And if you have been battling to break through and have prophetic dreams, this is the exact point that you need to start. You have been filling your mind with so much garbage up until now that the Spirit of God has not had the liberty to speak to you, because of all the junk that has been accumulated there.

If you have been looking to the Lord to really receive prophetic direction and guidance in your dreams, it could be that it is the garbage that is preventing it. The only way to get rid of that garbage is to saturate yourself with the Word; to speak in tongues continually and to release the Spirit of God from within you. As you do that the garbage will start being pushed out. And as the garbage is pushed out, so the water of the Word will be pushed back in. Eventually the stream that started off looking muddy, will become clearer and clearer, until finally you will receive those prophetic dreams of direction that you have been looking to the Lord for.

4th Category - Prophetic Dreams

Let's take a look at the category of prophetic dreams. The prophetic dream is experienced solely by the Christian. In such a dream, the message that comes up from your spirit, motivated by the Spirit of God, is to give you direction and guidance and insight to your spiritual walk. The prophetic dream is no different from visions, prophecy, a word of wisdom or a word of knowledge. If you have up until now flowed in any of those gifts you should be able to flow in dream interpretation, because a dream is simply a night vision. If you have received dreams and visions before and know how to interpret them, you will be able to interpret your own dreams.

Prophetic Dreams

12 Now there was a young Hebrew man with us there, a servant of the captain of the guard. And we told him, and he interpreted our dreams for us; to each man he interpreted according to his own dream.

13 And it came to pass, just as he interpreted for us, so it happened. He restored me to my office, and he hanged him

~ Genesis 41:12-13

Chapter 02 – Prophetic Dreams

3 Categories of Prophetic Dreams

There are three categories of prophetic dream that the believer can have. The first two are internal and are experienced by every believer, regardless of their spiritual gifts. The third type of prophetic dream (the external prophetic dream) is largely the domain of the prophet. I am going to lay a foundation here and will get into direct dream interpretation in a later chapter. So by the end of this series you will have a very good idea of how to take your dreams, interpret them; and then also take the dreams of others and interpret them and give them direction from the Lord.

1st Prophetic Dream: Internal Dreams

The first kind of prophetic dream that you can have is an internal dream. An internal dream pertains to you and to you alone. It involves your current spiritual condition with the Lord, where you are in ministry, and what condition your relationship is at with the Lord. This dream functions very much like the word of knowledge in that it relates to past and present events. It will give you an insight to your spiritual and soulish condition concerning things from your past, as well indicating the state of your current spiritual maturity or conflict.

An internal dream is about you and you alone. I am stressing this point here for a good reason. There is so much misconception in Christian circles, that because you have a prophetic dream, it must relate to somebody else. "If I dream about my auntie, it must mean that the dream relates to her, and the interpretation is for her." Not so.

An internal dream is for you, and all the symbols that are related in the internal dream pertain to you and you alone. Every character in your dream represents a part of yourself; a part of your emotions, a part of your mind, a part of your will, a part of your spirit, or a part of your flesh. We will go on later and I will show you how to take each character and identify what exactly they symbolize within yourself. The internal dream is about you and the message is for you from the Holy Spirit.

Identifying It

So how do you identify an internal dream? It is very simple. In an internal dream you are the main character. You are the star of the dream. You are involved in it and participating in it. You are active in whatever is happening in the dream. You are actively involved with the characters in the dream. This is an indication that your dream is internal.

Perhaps you have been having dreams lately where you are dreaming about being pregnant. This would perhaps apply more to a woman. Perhaps you have been dreaming that you have been pregnant or have given birth, will be giving birth, or are looking to get pregnant.

This could very well be the Lord saying that you have birthed something in your spiritual life. There is something new that He has given to you, perhaps that you have to birth through travail and pain.

Perhaps you have dreamt that the baby that you are birthing dies, in which case the Lord is saying, "Hey, this gift that I have given you is dying within you. You need to do something about it."

Perhaps you dream that your father comes to visit and tries to develop a relationship with you. In some cases your father could speak of the Lord, and the Lord could be saying, "Hey, let me in. I want to come and spend more time with you."

If you are an active participant in your dream, it means it is an internal dream and all the characters reflect a part of your own spirit or soul. As you identify which dreams are clearly internal, you will receive an insight into what is going on within you that you have never seen before. Often you face pressures and experience emotions in life that you cannot understand. Perhaps you have been feeling very melancholic lately or a deep weeping has come over you that you cannot understand. Your dreams could reveal to you the source of that rising emotion.

Very often as you face life, templates from the past are exposed and you find yourself facing emotions you cannot get a hold of. Be very aware of your dreams through a time like this, because they will very likely reflect what is happening within. At this time you could dream of characters of the past, which would reveal where the template was first formed.

Perhaps you will dream of your child being killed. I have two daughters and my firstborn (Deborah-Anne) has strong faith. When I dream of her, I know that the Lord is speaking of my faith. My second daughter (Jessica) is very soft and very affectionate. When I dream of her, I know the Lord is giving me a message with regards to my love. In one instance I dreamed that Jessica died. Now if you had to interpret this externally, you would give into fear and give the enemy license in your life. However I was an active participant in this dream. I dreamed that she was swimming and that she was gagged. And because she was gagged, she could not get air and drowned. In my dream I went to her and resuscitated her using CPR.

In the same dream, I dreamed that Deborah stood at the edge of the pool without putting on her floating device and just stepped into the water! My first reaction was to panic, but as I watched, she walked on the water! So what was the message from my spirit in this clear internal dream? If Jessica is my love and she was being gagged, it indicated to me that I had gagged my love! That I had stifled it and because I had stifled it within myself, it died. But yet it was resuscitated and so the Lord showed me that I would overcome this time of testing.

In the same instance Deborah, who was a symbol of my faith walked on water! This was a clear indication to me that I must step into the unknown and be bold, because by stepping out, I would walk on water and my faith would grow strong.

Perhaps you have been dreaming often of close family relatives or children continuously. As you identify them in your dreams, your night visions will open up to you in a way you have never seen them before. They will not only give you direction, but they will also give you hope for the future.

2nd Prophetic Dream: Internal Prophetic Dream

The second kind of prophetic dream is called an internal prophetic dream. While the internal dream indicates within you the current state of your spiritual condition, it operates very much like the word of knowledge in that it pertains to events present and past. However, the internal prophetic dream always pertains to the events in the future. Can you see the difference? They are both about you in that the internal prophetic is still about you, but it pertains to events in the future. You will still be the star character in the internal prophetic dream, but the events in the dream are a warning or a direction of what is going to happen in the future, while the internal dream is an indication of your current spiritual condition.

The Baker and the Cupbearer

A very good example in the Word of an internal prophetic dream would be of the baker and the cupbearer in prison when they met up with Joseph. You can remember the story, where the cupbearer came to Joseph and said, "I dreamt there were three bunches of grapes, and I squeezed the grapes out and gave the juice to the king and he drank of it."

Then the baker said, "I too had a dream in which I was dreaming that I had baskets of bread on my head. But behold the birds came and ate of the bread that was in the baskets."

Joseph said to the cupbearer, "What your dream is about is you. In three days the king is going to pass judgment, and you will be taken back into service."

The baker got all excited and thought he would get a positive interpretation too. But alas, it was not so great for him was it? Because Joseph turned to him and said, "I'm sorry to break it to you, pal, but in three days the king is going to have you hanged, and the birds are going to eat the flesh off your bones."

It was not a very wonderful interpretation, but a very good example of an internal prophetic dream. It pertained to the cupbearer and baker, but yet it also related to their future.

King Nebuchadnezzar's Dream

Another very good example would be when King Nebuchadnezzar had a dream and none of the wise men could interpret it. Of course, Daniel was called to interpret the dream.

The king said to Daniel, "Behold I saw a beautiful tree with branches that spread out, so that all the birds of the air came and nested in it, and all the animals came beneath. But then the tree was felled and a chain was put about it, and a voice from the heavens said that it shall eat grass and be as the oxen for a period of seven years."

King Nebuchadnezzar was confused until Daniel had to break the news to him and said, "You, O King are that tree. Your kingdom has increased, but you have become lofty and proud, and the Lord is going to cut you down. And He will make you to eat grass and be as a beast of the field for seven years."

Then Daniel went on further and said, "Repent to the Lord that this might not come to pass."

This is another very good example of an internal prophetic dream.

Identifying It

So how then would you identify an internal dream versus an internal prophetic dream? Firstly, like the internal dream, you are the star in 'the show'. It is also likely that you will dream of characters you are familiar with in an internal prophetic dream, but this is not always the case. What makes the internal prophetic dream stand apart from a straight internal dream is that in the prophetic you will dream of symbols that you are not usually familiar with. The internal prophetic dream comes from the Spirit of God to give you a message, and so you will dream of symbols from the Word of God. Now you may not be familiar with these symbols, so you would need to have a good knowledge of the Word. Having a good Bible program with a search capability on your computer will also help you look up symbols from your dream.

Here are two examples, one of an internal dream and then another of an internal prophetic dream. Both were submitted to me for interpretation by the same person, and they illustrate a clear example of what I have shared so far.

Let's take a look at the two of them and then make some comparisons.

Internal Dream: Second Hand Bassinet

"I was in my old apartment where I grew up. I was in my old room, but I was grown up and I had two children and one on the way. I stood in my room with my back to my old twin bed where I used to sleep and my eldest child now slept in that bed. In front of me was a white crib and a bassinet. The bassinet was in front of the crib closer to me. The crib was where my middle child slept.

Now the bassinet was empty because the child had not come yet, and I was preparing for that child to come. But the thing was this bassinet was old and yellow from use, broken down in some places. And my attitude was, oh we can fix it up and buy a new white cover and place it over it and no one will know the difference. Even as I dreamt I wondered to myself, why did I not just buy a new one, it's only about $30 for it. When looking at this dream I really did not like my attitude about that bassinet"

My Interpretation:

"This dream is internal and refers to your past and present spiritual condition. The fact that those babies were in a place representing your past, speaks of ministries you birthed in the past. In your dream they are already grown. But yet there is a new child on the way! As you look at your past and the methods you used for ministry in the past, you are trying to impose those past ideas and preconceived ideas on the new ministry the Lord is trying to birth in you.

However you cannot go back! What worked in the past will not work for this ministry that is about to be born! The methods and structures you used before, are not going to fit this new ministry. So my advice to you is to close the door to past ideas and methods and to look to the Lord for fresh ideas and gifts. Your gifts are going to change as will your entire structure. The Lord is about to give you a new vision and a new way of approaching it.

You are headed for uncharted territory. Put aside your comfort zone and launch out!"

Internal Prophetic Dream: The Key and the Sword

"I had two dreams the last couple nights. In the first one, I was holding a sword in my left hand. It was double-edged and razor sharp. I lowered my arm briefly to my side and though I felt nothing, when I looked down, there was a line cut on my leg (not deep) like it was so sharp!

Secondly, (next night) I went into a building I didn't recognize and there were others in army camouflage clothing as well. I/we came to a door that wasn't open. I looked in my right hand and there was a security key like the ones we use at work. I put the key in the door and walked through. I understand the symbolism of these two objects and wonder just where God is leading me."

My Interpretation:

"This dream is a clear internal prophetic dream. Although you are an active participant, the symbols used in the dream are not familiar to you. This dream has a future orientation and pertains to what you will be facing in the near future. It is very clear as to where the Lord is leading you my sister - He is leading you into the Prophetic Office! The sword speaks of the Word of God - but yet it cut you. *"For the word of God is living and powerful, and sharper than any two- edged sword, piercing even to the division of soul and spirit, and of joints and marrow..." Hebrews 4:12*

The sword is going to bring division to the joint and the marrow in your life, i.e. you are going to face a time of death and trial to prepare you for the calling in your life. This will mean laying the flesh on the cross.

The key speaks clearly of the Prophetic Office and this is where the Lord is taking you next. However, before He will trust you with that responsibility, you are going to face a time of death and division of your soul and spirit. In other words the templates you have, are going to be challenged and changed to accommodate the new anointing and authority the Lord wants to complete in you.

Have you had the opportunity to visit our prophetic school yet? If not I would say that this would be the right season for you to do so. Hang in there, you are about to embark on the journey of your life!"

Response:

"Thank you. The prophetic is the one thing I have always "told God" I was not interested in - it was for so-and-so, but not me, no way. However, I have known for several weeks now that there is a change in me and I feel a drawing in this direction. I feel like laughing with my God over this one. Love to you all in this glorious place."

Conclusion

Can you see at a glance the two different emphases of these dreams? The first displaying images of the past and present, the second having in it symbols that are out of character and unfamiliar to the student. Both dreams are also very straightforward with a clear message. I will be sharing more examples with you as we progress through this book as well as a table listed with the differences between the three categories of prophetic dreams. For now sit down and meditate on any dreams that come back to your memory and see which category they fall into. This is the first and most vital step in dream interpretation. Once you can place your dream in its category, interpreting the symbols comes easier as you allow the Word and revelation of God to flow from your spirit.

External Prophetic Dreams

*29 As for you, O king, thoughts came to your
mind while on your bed, about what would come
to pass after this; and He who reveals secrets has
made known to you what will be.*

*30 But as for me, this secret has not been
revealed to me because I have more wisdom than
anyone living, but for our sakes who make known
the interpretation to the king, and that you may
know the thoughts of your heart.*

~ Daniel 2:29-30

Chapter 03 – External Prophetic Dreams

3rd Prophetic Dream: External Prophetic Dream

The third kind of prophetic dream is the external prophetic dream. The external prophetic dream is mostly the domain of the prophet. It is not very likely that an average believer, not walking in the Ministry or Office of Prophet will have an external prophetic dream. Why? Because the external prophetic dream does not pertain to the dreamer, it is a specific word from the Lord to the Body of Christ, through His servant the prophet.

You are not likely, if you are not flowing in the Ministry or Office of Prophet, to have an external dream. But I am going to cover it here so that you understand the difference between the internal and the external.

Signs of External Dreams

The first sign that the dream is external is that you are not an active participant. You stand on the outside looking in, as if you are watching a theatre show before you, with the events being played out. If you have these dreams very often, it could very well be that the Lord has called you to the Prophetic Ministry, and you are not aware of it yet, because this is very much the function of the prophet – to receive directive words for the Body of

Christ. The Lord will use visions and dreams, prophecy, word of knowledge and word of wisdom.

Once again, being prophetic, this kind of dream has a future orientation. And once again the symbols in the dream are not necessarily who they are in real life, but rather symbolic of an emphasis group or archetype. They are symbols of various things. Nebuchadnezzar had a dream of the huge statue with the head of gold and the chest of silver, loins of bronze and the feet of clay. This is a very good example of an external prophetic dream, where the Holy Spirit moved on the king to give him an insight into the future.

Even though the dream was external and prophetic, the Lord was not speaking about an actual statue. So when you have an external prophetic dream and perhaps dream about the President or somebody particular in your church, or members of your congregation that you know, or even family members that you know personally, He is not necessarily speaking about that person specifically, but what they represent.

In Nebuchadnezzar's dream, the Lord was not saying that a huge idol was going to be built and that a stone was going to be rolled down a hill and the idol was going to be smashed. The idol represented the different nations that would rise up. And of course, the stone that rolled down the hill and smashed all the kingdoms to pieces was the Lord Jesus Christ, bringing His kingdom down to earth, which is us, the glorious church. So even in external dreams, the symbols are not who they are. They represent what they stand for.

Symbols

It could be that if you dream of your pastor that he represents a part of the church. If you have a good relationship with your pastor it could represent a leader in the Body of Christ. If you have a bad relationship with your pastor it could very well be that the Holy Spirit will use him as a symbol for the status quo. It depends on who you are as a person and how you perceive those characters, because the Holy Spirit will use characters that you are familiar with.

You see the Lord, in Nebuchadnezzar's dream, used an idol, because that is something he was familiar with. In his day they were familiar with building idols and statues to represent what they believed and signs of future events. It was part of their culture. So the Lord used that to give them an indication of what was going to happen in the future.

So the Lord will give you symbols. In both the internal and external prophetic dream He will give you symbols that you understand as an individual. This is why dream interpretation is so varied, because every human being is so varied. There are no rules set in stone that say, "Every symbol represents this." That is why we cannot go to the books of the world. The only book we have to refer to is the book of the Word. That is the only book we can refer to for the symbols in our dreams, because that is the foundation on which our faith is based and grounded in.

Recurring Dreams

What about those dreams that you have night after night? They have the same message and often the same emotion. While the surroundings in the dream may change, the events and the emotions remain constant. They are known as recurring dreams and every one of us has faced them more than once in our lives. On studying this I came to realize that recurring dreams indicate three different circumstances. The first type of recurring dream will reflect inner fears and hurts from the past that have not been dealt with. The second dream indicates that there is a message that the Lord is trying to get across to you and you are not grasping it. Then the third kind of dream is where you are living out your most passionate inner desires.

Inner Fears

Let's take a look now at dealing with fears. I have shared in the third chapter that those dreams where you wake up and the spirit of fear is attacking you, are not of God. However, there are cases where you dream out your own inner fears. This is not the same as that demonic fear. I am talking of an inner fear that has been plaguing you all your life. Perhaps it is a phobia. Perhaps you are afraid of the dark. Perhaps you are afraid of insects, snakes or dogs, and in your dream you are constantly coming into confrontation with that fear. It is as if every time you go to sleep you are constantly coming into confrontation with that snake, or that spider, or the darkness that you are so afraid of.

Perhaps you are coming into confrontation with people that you are afraid of. Have you ever had those dreams where you are walking around and you look down and you are suddenly naked? Those have to be the worst dreams. Or you are sitting in the bathroom and you look around and everybody is staring at you, and you are afraid. This is simply an internal dream. It is clearly internal and it is your spirit showing you very clearly that this is an area of your life that needs to be dealt with. This is something that needs to be given to the Lord, so that you may give it to Him as a petition and say, "Lord, please cleanse me of this." He can then bring healing to those templates where the fear occurred.

Dealing with the Past

What about those instances where suddenly as an adult, you will start dreaming of things that happened in your past? All that is really happening is your spirit is saying, "Here is an area that hasn't been dealt with."

When my little brother was about three years old, he fell into the pool in the middle of winter and my dad immediately dived in and grabbed him by the scruff of his neck. But after that, he had a terrible fear of water. Through the years it faded and then when he was eight he really started to enjoy swimming. He loved going out with the other kids and swimming, and yet he kept waking up saying, "I keep having these dreams of myself drowning." All that was happening is that with him beginning to swim again, it triggered off those fears from the past. He cannot even remember the incident. He cannot remember the time. But yet, it has been triggered to his memory and his spirit is saying very clearly, "Here is something that needs to be brought to healing. Here is something that needs to be dealt with in your life."

This is not the fear of the enemy. This is something that the Lord is exposing; an internal fear that has been in you for a very long time. And usually these dreams are recurring. Usually, when you have an inner fear, it will recur continuously.

There is another way that you can determine whether the dream is of the enemy or whether it is just the Lord prompting you to say, "This is an area that needs to be dealt with." You will dream perhaps the exact same dream over again, or even perhaps you will dream about the same fear in different circumstances. But all the time it will be the same emphasis, the same inner fear being brought out.

Healing of Fears

Then there will come a time when the healing dream will come where the inner fear will begin to rise up, and in your dream you will face that fear. I remember having a dream where I kept running away from something. I was not sure what I was running from, but in my dream I was running and running from this person in panic. Night after night I would have the same dream. Then the one night, in my dream, I turned around and faced that person. They disappeared and the running stopped.

Sometimes you need to face your fears in your dream. You can do that. You can face your fear, and it can be a healing dream, where the Holy Spirit can bring much needed rest to an area of your life that has been plaguing you for so long. It is really very, very simple. You do not need to go into a complex inner healing session with the Lord to bring healing to a past fear or template. Just submit yourself to Him and stand up to that fear, and He will give you the strength and the wisdom.

Get the Message

The second kind of recurring dream is those dreams where the Lord is trying to give you a message and you are not grasping it. This is clear when the king of Egypt dreamed of the seven cows and the seven ears of corn, and when Joseph interpreted the dreams, he said that the Lord has made the dream recur to denote the importance and the surety of the message.

I have come to experience this practically, as a lady who had suffered two very painful pregnancies is now pregnant again with more complications. She has placenta previa, which threatens her life as well as the child's. While in conversation with her, she mentioned in passing that she kept dreaming of a past relationship that she had entered into, in her days of rebellion. She felt the dreams were very unsettling as she had put this past behind her a long time ago, yet every night for months on end she dreamed of this person. The revelation came so clearly to me as she shared this. This relationship was the very reason why she had been struggling in her pregnancies!

As we addressed the issue and broke the links, the Lord reached in with His anointing to heal. It turned out that the person she had this relationship with was into the occult, and due to her involvement she had brought herself under a curse. The recurring dream was the Lord trying to get His message across to her.

Inner Desires

The last kind of recurring dreams are those that are simply a reflection of your inner desires. I remember a lady once sharing how she dreamed that she sang like an angel in her dreams, yet in reality she did not have a good voice at all. In her dreams, though, she could sing so beautifully and she used to wake up feeling so encouraged! Another example was of someone who had a deep desire to dance, but in real life had two left feet. Yet in her dreams she floated across the dance floor in the most graceful show of dance. She twirled and twisted and stepped as if she had been dancing all her life!

I would put this kind of dream under the heading of praise! These are the kinds of dreams the Lord gives us to encourage and bless us. It is in a dream like this that you live out and can experience those things you are incapable of doing in real life. I see these dreams as a blessing of the Lord to show us that with Him all things are possible!

Holy Spirit Interprets

Every person is unique and that is why I have entitled the message the way I did – Dream Interpretation by the Spirit – because the Spirit of God is the only Person who can interpret your dreams correctly. Not everybody, not even the wise men in the days of King Nebuchadnezzar, could interpret his dreams. Why? Because the dreams were given by the Spirit of God. And only one, seeking the Spirit of God, would be able to interpret those dreams.

That is why Daniel and the three other Israelite children were raised up as wise men in the court, because the Lord gave them supernatural wisdom to understand and interpret the dreams that He gave the kings of those times. This is very important for you to understand. You are an individual and the Lord is going to choose those things that are close to your heart.

Purpose of Dreams

What is the purpose of receiving dreams? Is it simply a means of fortune telling, or is it perhaps to give you direction? Perhaps it is simply so that you would know what is going on in your life.

Apply it

The objective of receiving an interpretation for a dream is that it is applied. As a prophet, when you receive an interpretation or a vision or revelation from the Word, the Lord would like you to share it for a reason; for the building up of the Body of Christ to the maturing of the saints. The Lord is not going to give you a prophetic dream for the fun of it. He does not hand it out like candy. It is not something that we do in our spare time when we have nothing else to do. It is not something super-duper. It is simply a means of the Lord revealing His will to His servants, so that they can take that will and then apply it to their lives.

A dream interpretation is empty until it is applied to your life. It is not there for entertainment. It is not there to tickle your ears. It is not just there to make you feel good inside. It is there to be applied for the maturing of the saints – being applied in faith, hope and love. That dream interpretation needs to be taken and applied practically, if it is internal, to your own life. If it is an external dream, it needs to then be applied to whom the dream is being indicated by.

Five P's In Dream Interpretation

9 Therefore give to Your servant an understanding heart to judge Your people, that I may discern between good and evil. For who is able to judge this great people of Yours?"

10 The speech pleased the Lord, that Solomon had asked this thing.

~ 1 Kings 3:9-10

Chapter 04 – Five P's In Dream Interpretation

5 P's in Dream Interpretation

As the Lord gives you a dream, whether it be internal, prophetic or external, you will be able to fit it in to one of these five headings, and as I break it down you will see clearly why. Those 5 P's are: petition, penitence, praise, proclamation and preservation.

First P - Petition

I have taken the example of Solomon, where the Lord God came to him after he was made king. And He said, "Solomon, what is it that you would have from Me?"

What did Solomon do? He said, "Lord, I am a child and Your people are vast. I need Your wisdom to judge such a magnificent people. You have raised me up on the throne amongst people whom I can't even count. Father, I need Your wisdom."

This was a prayer of petition. The Lord came to him in a dream and said, "Solomon, ask of Me what you will."

Immediately, Solomon came with a petition before the Lord and asked the Lord for wisdom. And his petition was granted. The Lord could very well bring out in your dream a realization where He is saying, "I need to pray about this. I need to go into intercession about this."

Perhaps you have been looking to the Lord for something. Perhaps you have been trusting Him for your healing. Perhaps you have been trusting Him for a financial provision. Whatever your need is, the Lord could very well come to you and say, "You've been asking Me the wrong way. You're praying the wrong way. Here, let Me give you some direction," and your dream could actually give you an indication of what you are lacking.

Perhaps you are lacking faith. Perhaps you are lacking hope. The Lord may, in your dream, give you an interpretation that says, "There is something wrong with your hope," in which case you go to prayer immediately, give it to the Lord and say, "Lord, give me hope." The Lord will give you a dream that will wake you up to the realization that you need to come before Him in prayer and get your answers.

Second P - Penitence

Then comes penitence. I love this example of Abimelech in Genesis 20:3. It says...

> *"But God came to Abimelech in a dream by night, and said to him, "Indeed you are a dead man because of the woman whom you have taken, for she is a man's wife."*

This is when Abraham decided to be really bright and say that Sarah was his sister instead of his wife. She was so beautiful that Abimelech thought that she would make a good addition to his harem.

The Lord came to him in a dream and said, "Abimelech, you're a dead man. You're touching My anointed," and Abimelech got the fright of his life. The first thing he did is he fell to his knees and said, "Lord, I'm a righteous man. Forgive me of this sin. I didn't touch her."

The Lord may, in your dream, bring about an interpretation that requires penitence. He could indicate that you have been harboring bitterness in your heart. He could bring about events and circumstances in your dream, as you sleep, that indicate that you have been harboring bitterness or pride, or that you have been involved in some sinful action that is not of God. In this case, the dream interpretation is very clear. Get on your knees and ask for forgiveness, and clear your heart before God.

Apply the Interpretation

Do you see how important it is to not just receive an interpretation, but to apply it to your life? Because like any other revelation, in fact even like the Word of God, unless that Word is taken and practically applied to your life, it is nothing but words, and it is nothing but pictures. It is not enough just to interpret dreams. You have to take that revelation and apply it to your life. And as you do that, the sword, which is the Word of God, will divide and cut asunder those things, which need to be removed.

As you apply the revelation you receive from your spirit, you will receive more and more, and so you will create in yourself a greater awareness to receive from the Lord.

He will then entrust you with more of His revelation. If you cannot take the simple revelation and interpretation of a dream and apply it in your life, the Lord is certainly not going to entrust you with the other gifts, such as the gift of discerning of spirits and prophecy, that you need to stand up and openly speak.

If you could just function in the measure that He has given you, even as small as this. If you can apply it to your life, you will begin a progress in the gifts of the Spirit and in walking in them. Soon the Lord will become very real to you, and you will begin to hear His voice clearly. You will have a greater awareness and clarity in what you hear. The dark sayings will suddenly become clearer and not so hidden in symbolism anymore, because you will start applying them.

It is like anything in this world. You need to take it and practice it. It is no good reading up on every weight loss book and aerobics book in the world, if you do not actually get off your butt and do some exercise! So do not just look for the interpretation that tickles your ears. Take the interpretation and apply it to your life.

If you are interpreting as a leader in the Body of Christ on behalf of another, take that interpretation and show them practically how they can apply it to their lives. The Lord did not give you the gift of interpretation, just to make people love you or to make you popular. He gave you the gift so that you may take it and teach people how to apply the interpretation to their lives, so that they may walk in victory and blessing and in the light that is our Christian walk.

Third P - Praise

The Lord sometimes likes to bless us with dreams that encourage us. He loves to give gifts to His children. As I said earlier, we know that even we who are sinful, wicked humans love to see our children overjoyed with gifts we give them. Just so, the Lord will give you a dream just to make you feel encouraged and to say, "You know what? You're on the right track. Hang in there. I'm pleased with you. You are a blessing to Me." He will give you dreams that say you are on the right path.

A lovely illustration is when Jacob fled from the presence of his brother, Esau, to go and find a wife for himself from amongst his father's people. On the way, he took a stone and put his head down and went to sleep. We all know the story. As he went to sleep he saw a stairway with angels ascending and descending and praising the Lord. And the Lord affirmed His Covenant through Abraham, Isaac and Jacob.

The Lord affirmed His Covenant to him and said, "You will become a great people." When Jacob woke up he rejoiced and built an altar to the Lord. And he said, "Lord, if You will put Your blessing and Your hand upon me, if You should have it that I could come back to this place, I will give you a tenth of all my earnings." Then he broke out into praise and he blessed the Lord, and gave his offering up to the Lord.

Sometimes you will have a dream that is put there just to bless you. It is simply to say, "My child, I am pleased with you. You are on the right track. You have done everything I've asked you. I love you, I care for you." And that just stirs your heart, and you will wake up rejoicing. Then take that joy the Lord has placed within you and pour it out to Him in praise and worship. Because as you pour out to Him in praise and worship, He then pours right on back to you, and you receive the wonderful love and blessing that He has bestowed on you.

Fourth P - Proclamation

Dreams are given for the purpose of proclamation. This is entirely the domain of the prophet. While petition, penitence and praise are something that every Christian can relate to their lives, proclamation is solely the domain of the prophet. Why? Because the prophet and also the apostle, have been put in the earth to speak forth the Word of the Lord, so that His Word may bear upon the natural surroundings and bring that Word to pass.

You need to be able to carry the authority of the prophet or the apostle, to be able to speak God's Word into the earth and have that Word bear on the natural. You need to have received the prophetic or apostolic mantle before you can take that interpretation, proclaim it and speak it into existence.

A very good example of this would be Daniel. If you read through the book of Daniel, you will see how he prophesies concerning the events of Israel, the current times and the nations that surrounded him, and of course, the famous 70 weeks. Do you know that Daniel received those all in a dream? He received them all in visions on his bed, he said. But yet he took those revelations and he wrote them down.

As he wrote them down, he was proclaiming into the earth the message the Lord had given him. As he sealed those words on paper, he was not just taking a dream and giving a great big foretelling. He was taking those words, and he was saying, "Let it be!" And as he wrote those words down, they went forth into the earth, and the circumstances were changed because of those words. Those words bore on the natural to shape it according to the Word that the Lord had spoken.

Apply it and Speak it

I found a lovely Scripture in Jeremiah 23:28-29 that explains it so well. It says:

> *"The prophet who has a dream, let him tell a dream; and he who has My word, let him speak My word faithfully. What is the chaff to the wheat" says the Lord. "Is not My word like a fire?" says the Lord, "and like a hammer that breaks the rock in pieces?"*

The Lord is saying it is not good enough to just dream and get a word. You have to take those words and you have to speak them forth into the earth. And this is likely to come in those external prophetic dreams where the Lord will say, "Thus says the Lord ..." where you receive a very clear direction from the Lord of what you need to speak and the actions that you need to make. And as you speak those words, and you act out those actions, you will be sending forth the Word of God into the earth like a fire that does indeed burn up the chaff, leaving the wheat standing.

Can you see how powerful dream interpretation can be when you apply it to your life? It is like any other revelation, but if you keep it within you, it is fruitless. If you do not share it and apply it to your life, the words are empty. Then you will come to say, "But the Lord said to me in 'this and this' dream that this would come to pass in my life." But if you did not share it, or if you did not apply that interpretation to your life, you cannot expect those circumstances to come to pass in your life. Because only once you have applied the revelation, can the revelation come to pass.

If you read through the whole of the Old Testament books of Isaiah and Jeremiah, they declare, "There shall be a virgin birth. A son is going to be born, and his name shall be Emmanuel, the great I Am." They were speaking into existence what was to come. They were saying, "There will be. There is going to be. Let there be!" and they spoke it into the earth. It came to pass. The Word of God brooded over the earth right like it did originally in Genesis and it caused the will of God to be made manifest in those surroundings.

Fifth P - Preservation

The fifth purpose of revelation through dreams is preservation. These are your warning or directive dreams in which the Lord will come to you and say, "There is a stumbling block in your life that needs to be avoided." These are internal prophetic dreams where the Lord will indicate to you very clearly what is going to happen. These are also very prevalent in external prophetic dreams, where the prophet may receive a warning for the Body of Christ or for a congregation in particular, a local church, or the Church Universal.

A very good example of an internal prophetic warning dream is with Joseph and Mary, where an angel came to Joseph and said, "You'd better get your stuff and move out, because Herod wants to kill the Child." The same warning was given to the wise men in a dream where the Scriptures say the wise men were warned in a dream not to tell Herod of the Child, so they went home by a different route.

They applied the interpretation of that warning dream and went home by a different route. If they had just received the dream and did not heed its warning, things would have turned out a little bit different for the Christian religion, don't you think? Things would have turned out very different. How important it is to apply the revelation the Lord gives us as servants of the Most High God.

Joseph received that warning and he packed Mary and Jesus up and he ran to Egypt. Then again he received a dream when the king in Jerusalem had died, and the angel said, "It is safe for you to leave," so they went away to Nazareth. They were warning dreams that were given.

Pharaoh and Joseph

You can see warning dreams right through the Scriptures. Another lovely illustration was in the days of Joseph, where Pharaoh had a dream about the seven sleek cows coming up from the river, and then seven lean cows after them, and the lean cows devoured the fat cows, but yet they still remained lean. Then he had another dream in which he saw seven ears of wheat, which were rich and ripe, and then seven scrawny ears of wheat, which devoured the rich ears. He did not understand.

Then of course Joseph gave the interpretation when he said, "Oh King, this is a warning of what will happen in future. You are going to have seven years of plenty, but then seven years of famine are going to come. And they are going to consume those seven years of plenty so badly that those seven years of plenty will even be forgotten."

Then Joseph said to the King, "King, if I may offer advice…" (he applied that interpretation).

"Choose for yourself one who is wise, that in the seven years of plenty he may gather a fifth of all the harvest and put it into storehouses, so that when the time of leanness comes you will not run out of food."

Joseph not only completed this application, but in the time of famine, Pharaoh ended up owning all the surrounding land and making himself very, very rich. What would have turned out to be a devastating time for the nation of Egypt, actually turned out to be one of the most prosperous times they ever saw in history. Because they had the finance and the food at that time, they received finance and resources in from all the surrounding nations.

There is not a single time in Scripture where the Lord gave a night vision to His servant, that that night vision was not applied. Look at Paul, in which he dreamt that a Macedonian came to him and said, "Please, come to us." He could have just left the dream there and nothing would have happened. But he rose up and said to the others, "I had a dream, and I believe the Lord wants us to go to Macedonia." So they packed up and went and applied the interpretation. He did not just leave it at that. You see how important it is?

CHAPTER 05

Dream Examples

---

9 Now the Lord spoke to Paul in the night by a vision, "Do not be afraid, but speak, and do not keep silent;

10 for I am with you, and no one will attack you to hurt you; for I have many people in this city.

~ Acts 18:9-10

Chapter 05 – Dream Examples

Here is a practical example of a dream posted to us:

Dream:

"I had arrived at an upcoming conference, and there were lots of people from all over the world who I had never ever met. And somehow, before I could enter in to meet the team and all the people that I do know, a man appeared to me outside of the door. He stood there blocking my way into the building, so I told him to move. But he didn't, so I began to hammer away at him in warfare, and then his face began to turn green and his tongue looked like a lizard's. I don't quite remember what happened after that, but after telling him to bow and to leave a couple of times, the dream ended (or of what I can remember) and I woke up this morning with a strong urge to fight and to intercede."

Interpretation:

Yes I believe the dream is an internal prophetic one. It would seem that the enemy would try to hinder you. It is a good example of a warning dream - it has no fear in it, but rather it has motivated you to action. The enemy is getting in the way of the direction the Lord has for you.

This could relate to the upcoming conference or your current situation. It would seem that the enemy would try and block your fellowshipping with us. Hang in there and resist him. The Lord has made you aware of his plans! Also keep an eye open for any open doors ok? The enemy can only attack if he is given license.

Reason for Revelation

Dream interpretation, like any revelation, is given to mature the saints. Paul gauges maturity in the churches by three yardsticks – faith, hope and love. In all the interpretations that you receive for yourself or that you receive for another, they should revolve around those three yardsticks at all times. They must build faith, they must build hope, and they must build love. Even a warning dream can give hope and direction. Any dream that produces fear, guilt and condemnation is not of God. But I am not going to go into that now, because in the third chapter we will discuss deception and the dos and don'ts of dream interpretation in detail. So I am just quickly going to go over faith, hope and love.

Faith

Faith is meant to bring direction and is meant to instill positive faith in the heart of the person that is receiving the interpretation. When Paul was in Corinth it says in Acts 18:9-10...

> *"Then the Lord spoke to Paul in the night by a vision saying, Do not be afraid, but speak, and do not hold your peace: For I am with you, and no*

man shall attack you to hurt you: for I have many
people in this city."

This night vision, or dream, gave Paul hope. This internal
prophetic dream gave Paul hope and faith, in that it said,
"Go for it, Paul, stop hiding. Stand up and speak and
nothing will harm you. I have many people here." Paul's
faith was built, and he rose up and went out into
Corinth, and he ministered the power of God, changed
lives, and he built the church at Corinth. It instilled faith
in his heart.

Another lovely example is Jacob, when he was working
for Laban, and he was getting ditched out of all his
wages. An angel came to him in a dream and he showed
him all the speckled sheep and the cattle. And he said,
"I'm going to bless you." That instilled faith in Jacob that
he was not going to sit in this position of servitude for
the rest of his life, but the Lord was going to raise him
up. And that is exactly what happened. He went to
Laban and requested the speckled cattle and rams. And
we know what happened after this. The Lord blessed his
action of faith, and he was encouraged to go forth and
do what the Lord had told him to do.

Hope

The revelation should instill hope in the heart of the
hearer. It will give confirmation. If you have been looking
to the Lord for something, asking Him for something,
very often you will have a dream that will give you
confirmation.

I found a lovely example with Gideon where he had gathered the men together and had sent half of them home, and now he had 400 men left. He said, "Lord I'm going to destroy the whole of the Midianite and Amorite camp with 400 men?"

The Lord said to Gideon, "Do me a favor and go down to the camp. I have a message for you."

Gideon went there and listened and heard two men talking in the Midianite camp relating a dream of a bush that came into the camp and all the tents were destroyed. And the one guy said to the other, "That is Gideon. He is going to overcome us." That instilled hope in the heart of Gideon. He went back, and he knew what he was going to do. He was going to succeed. It gave him a vision and he pursued that vision.

Here is a practical example of a dream that gave hope:

Dream: Swimming Pool / Candy

"This was a very short dream. I was dreaming that I was swimming in a swimming pool and I was enjoying myself. It was full of candy and very nice colors. It looked like the wrapping of the sweets that had nice colors."

Interpretation:

Your dream is an internal prophetic one, meaning that it relates to you and that the Lord is speaking to you of things to come.

Swimming in the pool refers to you moving into a new realm of the Spirit and operating in the anointing. The sweets are a wonderful picture of the Lord meeting your desires. He is not just interested in your needs - but your desires also! He desires to spoil you and give you those things that would make your heart glad!

I see here a spiritual and physical blessing on the way. Perhaps you have been looking to the Lord concerning moving into His anointing or have been drawing into a closer relationship with Him. Whatever the case, He is confirming to you that your prayer has been heard and that He is going to grant you both these desires!

Love

A revelation from the Lord should always instill love. A lovely example is of Peter, when he fell into a trance and Cornelius when the angel told him to go and get Peter to come and give him a message. Peter obeyed the direction that the Lord gave him and it opened up the church to the entire gentile nation. For the first time, the spirit and the love of God were made available to the gentiles and they were embraced into the Body of Christ. It encompassed them, and that love is now freely available to every person who would call upon the name of the Lord.

These should be our motivations in receiving an interpretation and in giving an interpretation.

You Can Have It

In conclusion, every born again believer is capable of dream interpretation. There are no exceptions. If you have the indwelling of the Holy Spirit and if you are born again by the Spirit of God, you can receive revelation via dreams. You also have the wisdom within and the gifts to interpret those dreams. The Lord is not going to give you something and then not show you how to use and apply it.

He is a faithful and a graceful God. If you desire in your heart to hear from Him, if you would just like to hear His voice and receive His direction in your own life instead of having to run to other people all the time to receive direction, it is available to you. You do not need to run to your local pastor or prophet or teacher to receive revelation for yourself all the time. You can receive it from the Lord directly, because He is dwelling right within you. You have the wisdom within you, and He is speaking in you all the time.

Do not think that you are deaf to His voice and that you do not have the ability or capability to hear Him. His law is written within us, in our hearts and on our minds. He is speaking to you all the time. If you would just reach out in passionate desire and in faith, the Lord will indeed not only grant you prophetic dreams and revelation, but He will grant you as well the wisdom to receive the interpretation and then apply it practically to your life.

Visions: Your Secret Conversation with God

17 That the God of our Lord Jesus Christ, the Father of glory, may give to you the spirit of wisdom and revelation in the knowledge of Him,

18 the eyes of your understanding being enlightened; that you may know what is the hope of His calling, what are the riches of the glory of His inheritance in the saints,

~ Ephesians 1:17-18

Chapter 06 – Visions: Your Secret Conversation with God

Knowing God's Will

Have you ever been at a crossroads where you desperately needed to know, "Is this the will of God? Should I go left; should I go right? Should I take up this job position; shouldn't I take up this job position? Should we have another child; shouldn't we have another child?" These may seem like very mundane questions, but yet in your personal life have you not desired to know the will of God for your life – for you today, personally, right now, for the simple decisions that you make day by day?

Perhaps you have looked at these great men and women of faith who stand up behind the pulpit and in front of big crowds and they seem so incredible. They share of these magnificent visions and great words of prophecy and revelation that they have received from the Lord, and you stand back and you say to yourself, "Wow. I wish that I was so important or that I was so spiritual that somehow I could hear from God like that. I wish that I were on their spiritual plane that God would speak to me in such tremendous visions and revelations."

Well, I have news for you today that if you are a part of the Body of Christ, no matter what part of the Body you are, no matter how small of a member you are you, Joe

Soap, Jane Doe, can hear from God for yourself. You, in your present condition, being saved by the Holy Spirit, born again by having accepted Jesus Christ into your heart, can receive visions and revelation. You can know what the will of God is for your life today. You can hear from the Lord for yourself. You can hear His voice, and you can see what He has planned for you.

This entire chapter will be about how you, as a child of God can hear from the Lord for yourself. You will be encouraged to enter into a relationship with God where the two of you have secret conversations. Where you and Him can enter into something so intimate that it will change and revolutionize not just your spiritual life, but the way you walk your natural life as well.

As I was looking to the Lord for a passage to begin with, He gave me Ephesians 1:17 and 18. I am going to spend a bit of time now breaking the passage down into its Greek so that you can get a clearer understanding of what God's will and purpose is for you when it comes to hearing His voice.

> *"That the God of our Lord Jesus Christ, the Father of glory, may give to you the spirit of wisdom and revelation in the knowledge of Him,*
>
> *The eyes of your understanding being enlightened; that you may know what is the hope of His calling, what are the riches of the glory of His inheritance in the saints,"*

Spirit of Wisdom and Revelation

I want to look first at what the spirit of wisdom is all about. What is this spirit of wisdom? I was fascinated when I looked up the Greek word for wisdom in the Thayers definition and this is what I found: 'The act of interpreting dreams and always giving the sagest advice; the intelligence evinced in discovering the meaning of some mysterious number of vision.'

I then went on to look at what revelation stood for. The Strong's definition there was, 'Disclosure of truth.' So the spirit of wisdom and revelation is the ability, by the Spirit of God, to know and understand dreams and visions and to receive for yourself, the understanding of the spiritual realm. This passage was written to the church of the Ephesians. It was not written just to those standing in ministry Offices. This was written to the entire Body of Christ, the entire member Body right down to the smallest toe.

Paul was not picking out select individuals and saying, "Well, I pray that you, John …" "I pray that you, James…" "I pray that you, Theresa, would have the spirit of wisdom." He was addressing this to the entire church. He was not addressing this to individuals. He was saying that they would all have spirit of wisdom and revelation. If you are a born again believer, you have within you the spirit of wisdom and revelation.

It says after that, '… in the knowledge of Him…' Who is 'Him'? Him is Jesus Christ. '…in the knowledge of Christ.'

I looked up knowledge and Strongs gave me: 'To become fully acquainted with.' So to be in the knowledge of Him means to become fully acquainted with Him. So not only do you have the capacity within you right now, today, wherever you stand, to receive wisdom from the Spirit and to receive revelation, but you have been granted the divine gift to become personally acquainted with the Lord of Hosts, King of Kings and majesty. You, little nobody, have the gift of becoming acquainted with and rubbing shoulders with, knowing personally and intimately, the Lord of Lords.

You do not get bigger connections in the world than that! Not just anybody can stand up and say, "Hey, I know God intimately. We chat. I'll give Him your number." Are you that bold as a child of God to say that? I am. And I tell you what, people are so taken aback that they listen.

"I know God. You mess with me, you mess with Him. I just want you to know that as we sign this business deal." You had better be sure that they will check the small print. They are not going to get themselves into trouble, because even unbelievers think, "Well, what if … just in case they know God, I'd better watch it with these people." It works. Are you bold enough to say that? You should be bold enough to say that, because according to the Word you have within you the ability to get personally acquainted with the living God who made the entire creation.

Visions – the Sight of Your Mind

Verse 18 goes on to say:

> *"The eyes of your understanding being
> enlightened…"*

What are the eyes of your understanding? I looked up
eyes and the literal translation is sight. I was fascinated
by what understanding stood for. It means figuratively,
the thoughts or feelings of your mind or the heart. Have
you ever read Scripture where it speaks about the heart,
and the feelings of the heart? It is speaking about your
mind. The eyes of your understanding means, the sight
of your mind.

That sounds a bit like a vision to me. That sounds to me
like you can see into the spiritual realm and know with
your mind what is going on. The 'sight of your mind'
means to be able to receive the spirit of wisdom and
revelation in your mind and for it to be enlightened so
that you can know what it is that the Lord is saying to
you at this time.

The Lord has a will and a purpose for you. The Lord of
Hosts, the King of Kings, desires passionately to have a
relationship with you. And according to His Word, it is
not only your free gift of salvation, but it is also your
right as a Christian being born into the Body of Christ.
You can know His will for your present-day
circumstance, and you can become fully acquainted with
the living God. And then you can act on the knowledge
of His will and have success in your life from day to day.

In this chapter, I will just be discussing visions, but there are very many ways that you can receive revelation from the spiritual realm and from your spirit. I am just touching on one area, because if I had to cover them all it would take too long.

Any Believer Can Receive

So to summarize, who can have a vision? Only those great men and women of God who stand behind the pulpits or appear on TBN? Are they the only ones who can have a vision? Do you have to be super-spiritual and go into a trance and perhaps be taken off to another land like John on the Isle of Patmos before you will be good enough for the Lord to give you a vision?

No. You just have to be born again by the Spirit of Christ to receive revelation from the Spirit of God. You have within you the Holy Spirit, the well of living water that springs eternally and gives eternal life and is constantly bubbling within your belly.

If you could just learn to tap into that, there is a wealth of revelation and wisdom for you to tap into anytime for any situation, for any need, for any desire, for any pain, loneliness or direction. It is there for you to receive here and now. And as I go through step by step on how you can tap into that inner resource I want you to open up and receive by faith that spirit of revelation, because it is yours by the Word of God. And if you will open your heart to it, by the end of this message you will indeed have received those gifts of revelation and you will be able to hear from the Lord for yourself.

The Purpose of a Vision

What is the purpose of a vision? Other than to receive direction for the will of God in your life, what really is the purpose of any of the gifts for that matter? It is really very simple – for the equipping and exhortation of the saints. For the maturing of the saints in faith, hope and love. You have heard this before. If you pick up any of our books or listen to any of our teachings you should know by now that the fruit of the Spirit, maturing of the saints, and anything that is produced by the spiritual realm is done by the agency of faith, hope and love.

That is why visions are given to the Body of Christ, that we may mature, that we may bear fruit. We are meant to stand as an example in this world, as a shining example of success, of boldness and leadership and ability. That we may receive that wisdom from God, who has all wisdom and knows and is all and who is in all. We should stand with that kind of power behind us, so that when we speak the world listens. When you open up your mouth to give advice you are speaking 'Jesus'. You are not speaking 'you'.

That is what revelation is for, to be the extension of Jesus, that this world may see a light as in the day of Jesus. As the Scriptures say, "And they saw a great light in Galilee." We should still be that great light in this world. That is what the gifts are for.

Take up what the Lord has given to you from the day of your salvation. It is in you now, it has always been in you, and it will continue to be in you. How much of it you tap into and how much you use, is up to you. Do you have what it takes? Does it burn enough in you? Because if it does, it is yours. Right here. Right now.

What are Visions?

By the biblical definition visions are, simply put, dark sayings. They are spoken in symbols and types and shadows. That is how the Lord speaks to us. We have covered a lot of this in the chapter on dreams and how the Lord speaks to us in dark sayings. He gives us symbols to interpret for understanding. Why is that? Why does the Lord always speak in shadows, types and symbols?

Why does He not say it plainly? Because the enemy does not understand symbols, types and shadows. The Lord speaks to us in our minds and He gives us those symbols and the enemy cannot read that. The enemy cannot read your mind. That probably shocked you, but the enemy cannot read your mind. That is why visions are so powerful. He cannot intercept the revelation given to you by the Holy Spirit that comes up through your spirit and into your mind. Sure enough, he can put external pressures on you and bring deception externally to bear upon your mind. But he cannot read the visions the Lord gives you. He cannot read the revelation that the Lord gives you unless it is spoken or acted out.

That is why it is your secret conversation with the Lord, because no man and no angel and no demon can know what the Lord is telling you. It is a very intimate communication between you and the Lord and it is one that every believer should be moving in and walking in every day of their lives, hearing from the Lord all the time. You should be hearing what He wants for you, hearing how special you are to Him. If you will open your spirit to Him, He will give it to you to the fullest measure that you can desire.

Receiving Revelation in Vision

How do you receive revelation in visions? Do you need to go into a trance? Do need to have open visions? Do things start happening and the earth shakes? Do you suddenly have to be put into suspension, and an image shoots up in front of your eyes and there it is?

No, that is not the usual way we receive visions. Perhaps in the Old Testament where they did not have the indwelling of the Holy Spirit it was necessary. Back then their human minds could not possibly comprehend the anointing and the power or revelation of God. But in this day and age we have the indwelling of the Holy Spirit.

While some people do have trance and open visions, it is by no means the norm. So if you think a vision is something super-fantastic that has to shake your whole world, then you are mistaken, because visions are really very simple. They are impulses from your spirit imprinted on your mind. They are really that simple. They are the pictures you see in your mind all the time.

Now if you are very artistic and draw, write poetry or write songs, this should be something very simple for you. You should think in pictures all the time. In fact, it is the way the Lord has made us humans. When we speak and describe things to people, we use illustrations. We are painting pictures with our words all the time so that people will understand what we are talking about.

The Lord does the same thing. When He wants to give you a message, what is the strongest sense that He is going to use to give it by? Think about it. Out of the five senses of taste, touch, smell, hearing and sight, which is the strongest? Sight! Sight is the strongest sense out of them all. So if you are going to receive revelation from the Lord for the first time, and if you are starting to become sensitive to the spiritual realm, the first thing that you will experience is visions. You will pick it up quicker because you are used to thinking in illustrations and you are used to watching TV. From a child you have heard the stories of Noah and the Ark and you have seen it in your mind. You have seen the ark, you have seen the animals and you saw the clouds. You have been trained to think in pictures from a very young age. So when the Lord speaks to you He is going to speak to you in pictures. That is all a vision is – a picture from your spirit.

Three Spiritual Functions

*These things we also speak, not in words which
man's wisdom teaches but which the Holy Spirit
teaches, comparing spiritual things with spiritual.*

~ 1 Corinthians 2:13

Chapter 07 – Three Spiritual Functions

There are three functions of the human spirit. This is standard human psychology. These three functions operate in everyone, saved or unsaved. The first is intuition, the second is spiritual wisdom and the third is communion. I have covered this in a lot of detail in our Pastor Teacher School, so I am just going to skim through the definitions very quickly for you here.

1st Function: Intuition

Intuition is something you should be familiar with. Apparently us women are supposed to be the best at it. I do not know, perhaps it is because we raise the kids and we can just 'tell' when they are up to something. Maybe that is what they call woman's intuition. But intuition is an inner knowing. You just somehow know. You do not know why you know, you cannot explain how you know, but you just know. It is a gut feeling. That is intuition.

2nd Function: Spiritual Wisdom

The second function is spiritual wisdom. Spiritual wisdom has a future orientation. It is an inner knowing with a future orientation. Unbelievers call it déjà vu. This is when you have a feeling that something is about to happen. You get this feeling in your stomach that somebody is going to phone, that car is going to turn in front of you, or you just know that that person will turn right or left. It is an inner knowing but it has a future orientation.

3rd Function: Communion

The third function is communion and that is the ability for us humans to sense other spirits. You can easily tell when somebody is down and depressed without them having to say a word. Now some people are really good at this, while others are pretty bad. But you can tell how somebody is feeling by them not saying anything. Have you ever considered that? Do you know that this is a natural function of the human spirit? You can tell when somebody is upset with you when they have on the biggest smile and they are being so nice and so friendly, but you 'know' that they cannot stand your guts!

How do you know that? You look at her and she looks friendly. You listen to her words and she is saying such good things. But you know that she is just putting it on. How do you know that? It is the spiritual sense of communion. You can sense the spirit of the people around you. Even unbelievers can do this. These are natural qualities. Even they can sense when you are 'putting it on'. It is a natural function of the human spirit.

Increase of Spiritual Awareness

Now when you become saved, these three functions become enhanced. Before you were saved your spirit was dead. It was dead to God. You did not function at all with an orientation towards God. You did not know God, you did not think about God. Your spirit was dead to Him. It was dead to the spiritual realm. There was no hunger or passion there. It was dead.

But the day you invite the Holy Spirit into you something happens. A life comes into you. The Holy Spirit comes into you. And suddenly there is an awakening towards God. There was a barrier before and now suddenly you break through this barrier into a realm that you have never experienced before. And if you think back on your salvation experience you know what I am talking about. The anointing that breaks through, the peace you felt or however you experienced it, something happened inside of you and you touched God for the first time in your life. For the first time He reached down and broke through that shell and He gained access to a place where nobody had been before.

That is the place that I am talking about deep down in your spirit and a new life was formed in there. As that new life was formed, a new awareness started developing about the Lord. And so the more you got into the Word and the more you fellowshipped with other believers, the awareness grew and grew until you started being able to sense the anointing. You started to be able to pick up revelation from His Word for yourself.

When you were saved something happened. But it does not have to stop there! The Lord just touched on a part of your life when you were saved, but you can expand on that. You can concentrate on that and you can live in that constant state of salvation every day of your life. The fire never has to die. His presence in your life never has to dwindle. It was there before; it can be there right now. And that is God's will for you right now. This is what He wants to communicate to you, and it is what He wants to tell you about. He wants to talk about you and Him and He wants to share His secrets with you, because you are very special to Him.

Spiritual Fruit

When your spirit is submitted to God, this is what happens with the three functions of the spirit.

Intuition Motivates Faith

Intuition, when motivated by the Spirit of God, produces faith. Are you starting to see the fruits and the maturing of the saints here? Faith is an inner knowing. When you allow the Spirit of God to take control of your life and submit to His will and start receiving revelation from your own spirit, the first thing that is will happen is that your faith will be stirred up. Your faith will be motivated because you will begin to see God's will for your life. You will not be looking at the physical realm anymore. Your eyes will be lifted up to the spiritual realm.

The Scripture says that we are to live by faith, not by sight. What does it mean? It means do not look to the natural realm. Put your eyes on the spiritual realm, because when you put your eyes on the spiritual realm you see past the obstacles that are in the natural realm.

I remember at one time when we were really battling financially. When I looked at things in the natural it seemed that there was this huge mountain ahead of us. The rent was due, the phone was due and the electricity was due. I am sure many of you can share your own stories in the light of our predicament. It was frustrating. No money was coming in. Nothing was happening. And every time I woke in the morning I saw this mountain looming in front of me. This mountain was huge and I could not get past it. I could not even pray. It was just so discouraging.

I finally went to the Lord and I closed my eyes and I said, "Lord, you've got to show me what's happening. I can't take this anymore!" He lifted me up and showed me what it looked like in the spiritual realm. And you know, from God's perspective the earth looks like a marble. So could you possibly imagine how tiny my mountain looked to Him?

He said, "Oh, is this the mountain of your problem?" He just sneezed and said, "There! It's gone!" It was really that simple for Him. It was so insignificant, He just needed to sneeze and it was gone. What was so big in the natural was so insignificant in the spiritual. This built my faith to press on and not long after this exact vision the Lord provided for us to have all our needs met! It is so our human nature, though, to keep our eyes on the natural realm all the time. Yet, that is where we miss it.

If you could take your eyes off the natural and put them into the spiritual and allow those visions from your spirit to be in your mind continually, your mountains will become molehills. What was impossible will suddenly become very possible. It will help you get up the next morning, and when you look at that mountain you will scoff at it, because you know better. You know something they do not know. You see something they do not see.

When your creditors are phoning you and saying, "Pay up or else," you can scoff because you know something they do not know. They might think you are a loser and they might think that you are not going to cough up, but you know better, because the Lord has shown you. You have seen what it really looks like.

The enemy can throw anything he likes at you, but when you know that you know that you know that God is bigger than this, there is nothing that can stand in your way. And there is nothing that the enemy can throw at you that you cannot overcome as a child of the Lord. And instead of running to the world every five minutes for solutions to your problems, you can stand as a believer and say, "I will not budge, because God has shown me…and God has said… and He is bigger than my circumstance. I saw it for myself."

You do not need to run to the nearest prophet or the nearest fortune teller to say, "What must I do? What is going to happen?" because you would have received for yourself from the Lord for your situation. This is available to you right now. Receive it by faith, because it is yours! You need to see your situation through God's eyes and you need to see it through vision in the heavenly realm. And when you do it is going to change the way you see everything. It will change the way you see your spouse. It will change the way you see your children. It will change the way you see your jobs and your responsibilities and your problems. It will revolutionize your life.

Spiritual Wisdom Produces Hope

The next function of the human spirit is spiritual wisdom. Can you guess what spiritual wisdom produces? It is future orientation and therefore produces hope. What would life be without hope? I guess it would be hopeless. That is what life would be without hope!

Spiritual wisdom produces hope, because when you have a vision for the future you can climb over any mountain. If you could only see the goal ahead of you or if you could see the outcome right now at the beginning of the race, you would know that the race is worth it to run. But the problem with a lot of Christians today is that they do not know that there is a goal at the end of this race. All they see is one stumbling block after the next one. They do not know that there is a goal. They do not know that they are victors.

I have news for you today. You are victorious through Jesus Christ who has saved you and does continually save you and will yet save you from every problem you will ever face! It is yours right now. You can know the end from the beginning.

Did you ever wish that you could go back in time with the knowledge you have now and relive your life? Well you can, only you can do it right now in the present day. You can know from God what your future holds and what direction you should take and apply it to your life now. You can see the end from the beginning, because the Lord is the alpha and the omega. He is the beginning and the end. He is at the beginning and the end of the race all at the same time.

If you would receive from Him you would know what your goal is. You would know what the outcome is going to be and you would know that it is worth it to push through. Then you can be victorious and confident in the way you hold yourself and in the way you present yourself to the world. You can know His will and you can live it every single day.

As I was doing this section, the Lord reminded me of how this whole ministry began. How at the beginning everything had fallen apart. We were stranded in Mexico, we did not have a friend or a family member anywhere near us. Here we were, and our income had been cut in one month. The person who had been supporting us cut us out entirely. Here we sat in Mexico. We could not speak the language so the people did not understand us. We had no family members even in the same continent and we had no money. That sounds like a pretty dreary situation.

Well, it **was** a pretty dreary situation! And if we had not looked into the spiritual realm and had **only** seen the

natural realm we would have seen what a dreary situation it really was. But... we did lift our eyes to the spiritual realm and the Lord showed us a goal. He showed us an international ministry reaching out, enabling and equipping millions of people. He showed us an international ministry that was going to revitalize the Body of Christ. A ministry that was going to change it, that would do things that would shake the core of the status quo church that had not been seen before.

Now that might sound like pride and it might sound like a vision bigger than you could perhaps comprehend, but that is the goal that the Lord gave for us. Here we were sitting helpless. We could not even pay the next month's rent. We did not know a living soul near us and the Lord showed us an international ministry reaching out across the globe into tribes and nations we had never even heard of before, to change their lives.

But I tell you something - it gave us hope. And as we walked up and down the beach and as the Lord began to burn this vision in our hearts, we cottoned onto this crazy idea to preach and produce tapes from the preaching. It was a crazy idea. Who knew? All we had was a video camera and it was just the few of us.

Who would be stupid enough to buy tapes from a bunch of people sitting in Mexico with a video camera? Who would have known that this very vision would have been the start of something so magnificent? Who knew that this small beginning was the start of the work of God in our lives that we could not have possibly comprehended

at the time? But because we saw the end from the beginning we knew the race was worth it to run. We knew that we would make every milestone that was set before us, because we knew the end from the beginning.

So we will continue to run that race and we will not stop running that race until we have reached the final destination. And I will tell you something else. Once we have reached that final destination there will be another goal for us to reach and we will reach that one too. This is what gets us up every morning – that goal ahead of us. This is also what you need from God for your life. You need a goal that will get you up every morning; that will make you want to get up every morning; that you cannot wait to get up every morning for. It is yours in Christ and it is yours right now if you will receive it from His hand.

Communion Produces Love

The third function of the spirit and the one that is the closest to my heart is communion. Three guesses on what the communion produces! So far we have covered faith and we have covered hope. Even my four year old could get this one right! Communion produces love. When you are in communion with the Holy Spirit, with the Lord Jesus Christ, you are looking into His eyes and He is saying to you, "You know what? I died just for you. Do you know why? Because you're so special to Me. You're worth it. I am so proud of you. I love you so much."

There is nothing you will not do for a person who says that to you over and over. With every nail they put in His hands and with every thorn they pressed into His head, those are the words that He said to you through time. They are still echoing through time and will continue to echo through time until the end of the ages.

There is power in communion with the Holy Spirit, our wonderful God, and our Lord Jesus Christ who gave His life for us. To know His will for our lives is powerful, but to know His love is revolutionary. It will change your life. It will change your heart. It will change your outlook. You will die for Him. You would want to die for Him.

Do you know that you can know God like an intimate lover? You can. And do you know that God Almighty wants to know you like an intimate lover? He wants to have secret conversations with you twenty four hours a day, every waking moment. Every time you close your eyes He is there, He wants to be there. He wants you to hear what He is saying to you. You can have it. It is yours. You can be talking with Jesus twenty four hours a day and falling in love with Him anew and deeper every single day. He can also fill every need in your heart if you will open it to the spirit of revelation and wisdom, which is yours.

Take Him with You

As I was looking for examples through the Scriptures I realized something quite interesting. Whenever Jesus opened His mouth to speak, He spoke in parables. What are parables? Are parables not symbols and types and shadows? Are they not painting pictures with words? If you want to talk to Jesus, He is going to still be speaking to you in parables. It is the way He talks. It is the secret language of God Himself. Even on this earth Jesus spoke in pictures and types and shadows. He painted pictures for the multitudes continually. He did not open His mouth without painting pictures and He is still doing it today, if you will quiet your spirit down enough to hear Him. He is still talking in parables.

Jesus often said to His disciples, "I only do what I see My Father do." And if they tried to push Him to do something He said, "No, I haven't been given the go-ahead from the Father." Jesus lived in vision twenty four hours a day. He was watching the Father for every footstep that He made. He did not move without seeing the Father do it first. Jesus is an example of how we should be living our Christian lives. You should not be making a move without knowing what the Lord wants. You should be saying, "Hey Lord, what do you think? Should I get the blue one or the red one?"

Does that sound crazy? Does it sound crazy to take the Lord Jesus clothes shopping with you? I do not think it is so crazy, because wherever Jesus went He took the Father with Him. And whatever He saw the Father doing, He did Himself. There was not a move that Jesus made without seeing what the Father did first. He was talking to the Father all the time and seeing what He was doing all the time. This is what we need to be doing as well – seeing what He is doing, seeing in the Spirit continually.

That is the power of visions – seeing in the Spirit continually the plan God has for your life.

"God, do you want this person healed? Lord, do you have a word for this person? Lord, I wish you would give me something to say that will pick this person up because they are so depressed. Give me the words."

Receiving Visions

*Then the secret was revealed to Daniel in a night
vision. So Daniel blessed the God of heaven.*

~ Daniel 2:19

Chapter 08 – Receiving Visions

It is all in your spirit. You have it. It is yours. So let's get to some practical applications. How do you receive visions? We have already discussed how it comes up from your spirit and puts an imprint on your mind. It is really very simple. You are receiving impressions from your spirit all the time. We have already covered in dreams how when you go to sleep those impressions come out of your spirit in your sleep and you dream them. But this also happens to you during the day. The only difference is that at night all your other senses are suspended so that you see them clearer. You are getting impulses from your spirit twenty four hours a day. You just do not stop long enough to listen to them.

Quiet all your senses. Go and find yourself a quiet little room somewhere where there is nothing to distract you. Then close your eyes. What pictures come to your mind? I am not expecting you to get anything super-duper, but what pictures come to your head? Write them down. You will get a couple. You just had a vision. It is that simple. It is impressions from your spirit. The more you just let it go and allow the Holy Spirit to speak to you, the more of those impressions you will receive. Soon it will come to the stage that wherever you are walking, or whatever you are saying or doing, you are receiving those impressions from your spirit.

I live in visions constantly. I was saying to the team the other day that I cannot even sit down and write an administrative letter without getting a vision. It is because I say, "Lord, what should I say to this person?" and He gives me a vision, and so I tell them. I cannot even do business without receiving visions. I say, "Lord, should I make this decision or should I make that decision?" and He will give me a vision. I live by it continually. There is not a thing that I do; there is not a conversation I am in where I am not using illustrations from visions that are popping up in my mind continually. And the more you take note of them the more of them you will see.

That is how we should be living. We should be receiving impulses from our spirits all day. Our spirits should be more alive than our human appetites for food. We should be hearing from God more than we hear from our stomachs. That is where the Body of Christ should be and you can be there. You do not need to be on a super-spiritual plane. You can be there right now.

Increasing Your Capacity to Receive

I want to discuss now how you can increase your capacity to receive visions. There are two ways. The first way is by pushing in the Word. The second way is by pouring out the Spirit.

The Word

If you want to receive visions that are of the Spirit of God it would be a good idea for you to read His handbook first on how to have visions. Pick yourself up Genesis to Revelation. That will give you a good enough background on receiving visions and interpretation by the Spirit.

Push the Word of God down into your spirit. Now, I am not talking about just reading through the whole Bible. There have been men and women who have read the Bible from beginning to end and still do not understand it and still live like the devil himself. So just reading it is not enough.

I am not being hypocritical and am not trying to speak against the Word of God in any way, do not get me wrong. But it is possible to simply read the words and for them not to sink in. It is possible to read the Bible over and over again and for your life not to be changed. Why? Because it does not go any deeper than your mind, the Word of God needs to get deeper than your mind for it to come out of your spirit. You have to push the Word down into your spirit.

Use Pictures

How do you push the Word into your spirit? Well think about it, how does revelation come up? It comes up in visions from your spirit does it not? So push it down in visions as well. How do you do that? Take yourself a passage, any passage, it does not matter. You can even pull out your favorite. Now, when you read it, do not simply see the words, "If you abide in Me and My words abide in you..." Instead of just seeing the words, see the pictures behind the words.

What do you see when you read that Scripture? *"If you abide in Me, and My words abide in you, you will ask what you desire, and it shall be done for you."* What picture comes to your mind when I quote that to you? For me, I see the Lord Jesus holding me as if I was a little child. He is my daddy and I am sitting on His lap. I am abiding in Him (He is holding me), He is abiding in me. Then I see Him picking up a gift like He had a surprise for me behind His chair. He picks it up and hands it to me, and I am so excited. I ask whatever I wish and it is done for me.

That is what I see when I quote that Scripture. I see myself on my heavenly daddy's lap and He gives me surprises, because He knows the desire of my heart. That picture will stay with me forever. Now you may not remember the words of that verse. In fact, you have probably already forgotten them. But I tell you what, that picture will go with you to your grave. You will never forget it!

Now the next time you are in prayer or the next time there is somebody having a hard time, I will tell you what will pop out of your spirit. That very picture! And so you will say to that person, "You know, there is a Scripture that says if you'll just let the Lord hold you and if you'll just be with Him, He'll help you through anything and He will give you the desire of your heart." You may not be able to quote it word for word, but you will know

P a g e | **100**   Chapter 08

what it means and you will know that it is there, and it will remain with you.

Whenever the Lord wants to bring that Scripture to your mind or whenever He wants to say, "Hey, I'm holding you in this one," that picture will come to your mind. And so you and Jesus will have this little secret conversation, because only you and Him know what you are talking about. He is going to pop that picture into your mind and He is going to say, "This is what I mean," and you will understand what He is saying, because you pushed that picture down there in the first place. So you will begin having secret conversations with the Lord Jesus, and that is what it is all about, isn't it – having that intimate secret conversation with the Lord.

Much Dreaming

As you start pushing the Word in, as we have discussed in dreams, all the garbage will come out. Now that garbage will pour out into your dreams. Persevere with it though. Take your favorite Scriptures, visualize them and push them down. Quote them. Get them into your spirit. Get them deep within your mind. Do not just understand them. See them, smell them, feel them, taste them. Make it something real in your life. Do not make it a couple of words on a page. Do not make it something that your pastor quotes at you from the pulpit. Make it something that means something to you. Make it yours!

Take the Scripture and say, "This is my special secret from God just for me," because when it is yours, then it is going to mean something to you. And when it means something to you it will build your faith, it will build your hope and it is will restore your love.

Pour out the Spirit

The next way to increase revelation is by pouring the Spirit out. How would you do that? How do you take the stream that is within your belly and pour it out? By speaking in tongues (which is the language of the Spirit) and also by journaling. By speaking in tongues your spirit is speaking with God continually. As you do that, the rivers of living water that have been clogged and closed up within you for so long are suddenly going to be released through your mouth.

What will happen is that a little bit of shaking will go on in there. All the Word that you have been pushing down in there for some time now will start coming out again. As you start speaking in tongues over and over and releasing, something will start to happen. You will start feeling what feels like butterflies in the pit of your stomach. It will feel like a bubbling happening and that bubbling will start coming out of your mouth.

As it starts coming out of your mouth and as you persevere, the visions are will start coming forth. If you will take note of them and stop for long enough to realize that you are actually having visions, you will be surprised how rapidly they come. And the longer you spend praying in tongues, the more visions you will receive. They will probably come faster than what you can cope with.

Journaling taps into that same stream. Sit down with a pen and paper in a quiet place and have your secret conversation with the Lord on paper. Just begin by talking with Him and by pouring out your heart. Then as the pictures start to come, write them down and let the words flow freely from deep within. Do this daily and you will be amazed to see the direction and revelation the Lord will give you for each day.

Into the Secret Place

Now as you continue with this, what will happen is that you and the Lord will be able to hide away in that secret place and He will begin to tell you things that will blow you away. He will tell you secrets. He will tell you special things just between you and Him. He will take you to a secret place where it is just the two of you. He will take you where you are standing next to a river. The grass is green and it is a beautiful day, and there is a huge tree hanging over the river. He will sit there with you and He is going to chat. You are going to hear Him, you will be able to talk back to Him, and then He is going to answer you. Very soon you will find yourself falling head over heels in love with the Lord Jesus.

Do you want that? As I shared that picture could you see it? Could you hear the water? Could you smell that fresh air? Do you want that? You can have that! It is what

Jesus wants for you. He wants to take you there. He wants to take you to that secret place where the world is left behind, where the heartache is left behind, where the pain and the frustration and the anger and everything you have to face every day is left behind. He wants to take you to a realm where there is no shadow of turning, where there is no sorrow. That is where He wants to take you, and He wants to take you there right now, if you will let Him.

Release the Blockages

In conclusion I am going to end with a passage from Matthew 13:14-16

> *"And in them the prophecy of Isaiah is fulfilled, which says: 'Hearing you will hear and shall not understand, and seeing you will see and not perceive;*
>
> *For the hearts of this people have grown dull. Their ears are hard of hearing, and their eyes they have closed, lest they should see with their eyes and hear with their ears, lest they should understand with their hearts and turn, so that I should heal them.'*
>
> *But blessed are your eyes for they see, and your ears for they hear."*

Perhaps your heart has become a bit like stone. Perhaps it has come to the stage where you cannot feel the presence of the Lord anymore; where you have forgotten what His voice sounds like; where you have forgotten what that gentle breeze feels like blowing over your skin. You have forgotten what it felt like to be born again. You have forgotten the fire and forgotten the passion, and you have faced so many hard times that your heart has become hard, your ears do not hear and your eyes do not see anymore.

The Holy Spirit is with you right now and He wants to break through that if you will open up to Him. If you will do this, He has waiting for you a face to face relationship where He can show you His will for your life. He can reveal to you the secrets of His Kingdom and of the spiritual realm.

That is the power of receiving visions from the Spirit of God. I want you to close your eyes and I want you to open your spirit and receive from the Lord for yourself right now. I am going to release the anointing on you and I want you to receive it, because the Holy Spirit is here with you right now. He is brooding over your heart just as He brooded over the waters on the day of creation.

Can you already feel the stirring in your belly? Can you feel that churning inside that says, "God I want more of you. This isn't enough. This isn't enough anymore. I want to see You, not in a dark glass. I want to see You clearly. I want to see Your image in daylight. I want to know You like I know my spouse and my children. I want to know you closer than breathing." Does it burn in you? Because if it does, He is there with you right now to give you your heart's desire.

"Father I pray that You would touch Your people; that you would open up the eyes of their understanding; that You would open up their ears to hear. Holy Spirit be released on Your people. Let them hear Your voice even now as it begins to whisper in their ears. Open their hearts that they might see the visions that You have for them; the visions of the future; the visions of hope, of faith. May they know Your love and see You enfolding them in Your arms.

Father I pray that You would just overshadow Your people right now. For that soul right now that is just aching to know You, reveal Yourself to them in a very special way. That you would enter into that heart and into that life and give them the revelation that they are special to You. That you have a work for them, that You have a place for them in the Body of Christ. They do not stand alone, but they are one member of many members and part of a magnificent and glorious Body. Lift up Your people Father. Lift them up to the place where they should stand, in a place of victory, in a place of glory as an example to this world.

I send forth Your light right now and let it shine. Let it shine in all its glory. Thank you for melting that heart right now in Jesus' name. From your head to your toes you are being changed right now. Your heart is being rearranged and you are never going to be the same again, because the Spirit of God has anointed you and is upon you and He will raise you up. For He will indeed raise you up, and you will indeed speak His Word to the nations! Thank You Father!"

Nightmares, Deception and Demonic Dreams

15 Then a spirit passed before my face; the hair on my body stood up.

16 It stood still, but I could not discern its appearance. A form was before my eyes; There was silence; Then I heard a voice saying:

17 'Can a mortal be more righteous than God? Can a man be more pure than his Maker?

18 If He puts no trust in His servants, If He charges His angels with error,

19 How much more those who dwell in houses of clay, whose foundation is in the dust, who are crushed before a moth?

~ Job 4:15-19

Chapter 09 – Nightmares, Deception and Demonic Dreams

Identifying Deception

In this chapter we will be looking at the 'not too nice' side of dream and vision interpretation. My hope it that this will not discourage you, but rather encourage you to look for the Word of the Lord in your life, and to avoid those words and negative impressions that are not of the Spirit of God. This will promote you to maturity, to strength, and to faith, hope and love in the Lord.

I would like to begin with Job 4:15-19

> *"Then a spirit passed before my face; the hair on my body stood up.*
>
> *It stood still, but I could not discern its appearance. A form was before my eyes; There was silence; Then I heard a voice saying:*
>
> *'Can a mortal be more righteous than God? Can a man be more pure than his Maker?*
>
> *If He puts no trust in His servants, If He charges His angels with error,*

How much more those who dwell in houses of clay, whose foundation is in the dust, who are crushed before a moth?"

I have chosen this passage as our key passage because it displays very clearly all elements of deception. It displays fear, it displays condemnation, and it questions the Word of God. All of these are very clear signs of deception.

3 Categories of Deceptive Dreams

I will begin by breaking down deception into three main categories. Those will be: Dreams that you have where the events actually occur; those dreams and visions you receive where that revelation is false; and finally when the Lord truly does give a Word, but then the revelation is misinterpreted. Once again, as I covered in the first chapter, even though dreams are something that you have when you are asleep, they are very much like any other gift of the Spirit. They are simply night visions.

What I will share in this chapter does not only apply to dream interpretation, but it applies to any revelation that you receive from the Lord. As you start out, the possibilities are stronger that the Lord will begin speaking to you in dark sayings in your dreams. So as you begin to apply these principles in those dark sayings, and then move into a clearer understanding of His voice in visions and direct words of knowledge, wisdom and prophecy, you can continue to apply these principles to your strengthening, maturing and growing in the Lord.

1st Category: Events That Actually Occur

The first category of deception occurs where a person dreams of horrific events that actually happen. These usually fall into the external type of category where you watch an event from the outside, and it looks very much like an external prophetic dream pertaining to somebody else. A typical situation would be of you dreaming of someone's death; dreaming they are having a heart attack or stroke; dreaming that a child dies. These all fall into this category.

I found a good passage in Jeremiah 29:8-9 which says:

> *"For thus says the Lord of hosts, the God of Israel: Do not let your prophets and your diviners who are in your midst deceive you, nor listen to your dreams which you cause to be dreamed.*
>
> *For they prophesy falsely to you in My name; I have not sent them, says the Lord."*

I have had a lot of experiences where prophets in particular have written to me with dreams that they have had about actual occurrences. One such incident was when a dream was submitted about a certain child that had been mutilated in a car accident. The lady who had the 'dream' woke in a state after dreaming of a boy being hit by a truck and the remains that were left. She woke and even continued to see the events in vision. She looked out her window and 'saw' this child mutilated and could still hear his cries in her ears. She described him right down to the clothing he was wearing. The part that concerned me was that the very next day she was called to the hospital, as her sister's son had been involved in a serious accident. When she went to see the child, he was wearing the same clothing she saw in her dream. The child died.

Well, I do not think you even need the gift of discerning of spirits for the hair to stand up on your head, to know that this is not of the Lord.

Divination

Such dreams and revelation in the Scripture are commonly known as 'divination'. If you look up the word divination in the Hebrew you will find the words related to it are 'soothsaying and foretelling', neither of which are from the Spirit of God. God does not foretell by soothsaying. He declares His will to His prophets and to His people, so that they might speak forth His Word into the earth and bring His will to manifest in the natural. The Lord is not in the business of fortune telling for your common interest and knowledge. He is not in the business of foretelling for self-promotion and financial gain. That is not how the Lord works. Unfortunately, this is something that has become very prevalent today as people are starting to move into the gifts of the Spirit.

We have received many applications since we launched the Prophetic School, where an applicant will say very clearly, "I am a prophet, because I dream of things before they happen. I have received this gift from God, because even before I was saved, I received revelation about people and personal information. I know what's going to happen to them before it does. I dreamt of when my brother died, my auntie died, my best friend died. I dreamt of this before they died."

This revelation is NOT from the Spirit of God. And if you are experiencing this type of revelation, I want you to know right now that this is a spirit of divination. It is a spirit of witchcraft. It is of Satan, and you have given the enemy a hold in your life somewhere, that he has been able to step in and deceive you, coming in the guise of the revelation of the Lord.

The Lord is not in the business of promoting death, or promoting fear and doubt and condemnation. And these are all elements that divination promotes. You need to be very clear on this, particularly if you are using this training method to interpret the dreams of others. When somebody comes to you saying, "These dreams actually happened," particularly if they are negative, or if they are speaking of death and circumstances that have occurred that are negative, you need to be very wary, because this is not how the Lord works. He does not work in divination and soothsaying and foretelling. He works to the building up of the saints, in faith and in hope and in love, bringing His people to a place of maturity and relationship with Him.

A good example of divination in the Word is in Acts 16:16 where you find Paul being followed around by a woman with the spirit of divination, in which she was declaring, *"These men are the servants of the Most High God, who proclaim to us the way of salvation."* It sounded like she was telling the truth, didn't it? I was always frustrated when I read that Scripture because I said, "How could this woman have been a false prophet when she was speaking the actual truth? They were servants of the Most High God. Is that not what she was saying?"

But if you read between the lines she was saying, they are proclaiming a way to the Kingdom of Heaven. So in amongst that truth was a word that was shifting the people's emphasis away from one true God. And you know the story of how Paul turned around and told that spirit of divination to come out of her in the name of Jesus. And he caused a mighty ruckus in that city because of it and ended up being arrested.

But you see how the deception is, in that Satan comes as an angel of light. It looks so much like a revelation from the Lord. It looks so much like it could be truth. In fact, did it not happen that if you had a dream that somebody died and it did happen, isn't it obviously of the Lord? Just like this woman was saying, "They are servants of the Most High God," was she not speaking the truth?

Satan comes as an angel of light and you need to get into a relationship with the Lord Jesus where you can discern what is of light and what is of darkness. Only one called to the Prophetic Ministry can stand in the Office of Prophet and declare forth the Word of the Lord for the future. And only a mature prophet is called to stand up and speak this Word for the future. The Lord will not reveal it to you if you are not standing in that Office. If you have not even moved into the Prophetic Ministry and you are having these strange and horrific dreams of things really happening, I would sit up and take notice, because it is not from the Spirit of God.

2nd Category: False Revelation

The next from of deception comes as false revelation. This is slightly different from divination in that the revelation is obviously false. It is simply a lie, a deception, an accusation put in the mind of the receiver that does not come to pass and is truly a false revelation. It is entirely possible to have a dream in which the interpretation is totally out of order.

A very good example of this is Zechariah 10:2

> *"For the idols speak delusion; the diviners envision lies, and tell false dreams; they comfort in vain. Therefore the people wend their way like sheep; they are in trouble because there is no shepherd."*

False interpretation scatters the flock. It brings confusion, it brings doubt and it brings discouragement in the heart of the receiver. It does not leave them with a direct path to follow. They are put on the wrong track. When coming to the Lord to receive revelation from a dream or vision that you have a received, as a very clear guideline, look at yourself first. See first if the revelation applies to you, before you stand up and start proclaiming that it is for everybody else. You are still on safe ground when you are looking at yourself and saying,

"Does this apply to me?" But when you start speaking it forth and it is not of God, you will find yourself in a situation where the word you spoke does not come to pass. It is a deception and you will be leading people astray.

People think that because the Lord has given them a gift to speak forth His revelation, they can just stand up and declare it without stopping for a moment to see if it lines up with the Word of God and the Spirit of God, before speaking it forth. Always line up everything you receive from your spirit with both the Word of the Lord and the Spirit of the Lord, because the Lord Jesus will not contradict Himself. As we go on I will give you some very clear signs to watch out for in your dreams, that will indicate whether the revelation is false or deceptive.

3rd Category: Misinterpreting Revelation

The third form of deception lies in the misinterpretation of dreams and visions. Misinterpretation is when the Lord will give you a revelation that is indeed a pure revelation from the Holy Spirit, but that revelation is then interpreted incorrectly. Perhaps the Lord has indeed spoken and moved on you, perhaps by giving you a symbol, a picture, a circumstance to meditate on that is a true revelation. But what happens is that the person in question takes that revelation and twists it to suit the understanding and logic of their own human mind. When you start messing around with the revelation that the Lord has given you, and start applying your own logic and your own common understanding and knowledge of the world, you are starting to get into trouble.

The greatest mistake I have seen in this area is when a person receives a dream that is clearly internal and they interpret it externally. Because when they look at the interpretation of the dream they think, "Well, this couldn't possibly be for me. The Lord couldn't possibly be saying I am out of order. This word must be for the church." So they stand up and proclaim this magnificent dream that is clearly relating to them, and they relate it to the Body of Christ or to their congregation, and then they use it as a whip of revelation.

You need to be very discerning. When you are the star character of the dream, it is internal. Do not take an internal dream and interpret it externally to meet the desires of your own heart and your own flesh and to say, "Thus saith the Lord…" especially when you are moving in revelation for the first time and you have only just begun to receive revelation from your own spirit. This is a very clear guideline to follow.

I remember one incident where a dream was submitted to us for interpretation and the person in question had included their external 'magnificent' interpretation. Now, this person was particularly against the revival movement. She was not exactly in agreement with the manifestations and concentration and the hype on the revival movement that was sweeping across the nations.

So she took this dream, which was very clearly internal, of an incident where she came to a bar and there was a person sitting there reading the Word. The clear internal interpretation was the Spirit of God saying to her, "You need to go and receive of My joy and My Spirit." It had a very positive connotation. The Lord was saying, "You need to get into this revival anointing. You need to get in there where My Spirit is flowing, so that you can taste of it and see that it is good and have joy in your heart, and move into the next stage of your ministry."

But because she had the preconceived ideas in her mind of what she stood against, she interpreted it to mean that the church was running after this as if it was a worldly thing; as if it was something that was sinful and looking after the lusts of the flesh. She interpreted it totally externally and so used it as a whip against the revival movement, which she stood against.

Do not take the revelations the Lord has given you and add your own dogmatic ideas and preconceived ideas to it without first measuring it up with the Word of God along with the witness of the Holy Spirit. Remain teachable. Keep your heart open, and allow the Holy Spirit to change you. For as long as you keep your heart open to Him in contriteness and humility, He will not stop from pouring His Spirit into you and encouraging you, and leading you in the direction that He wants you to go.

It says in Jeremiah 23:36

> *"And the oracle of the Lord you shall mention no more. For every man's word will be his oracle,*

> *for you have perverted the words of the living*
> *God, the Lord of hosts, our God."*

Do not take the words that the Lord has given you and
pervert them with your own words and your own
dogmatic ideas and doctrines.

The Signs of Deception

*That we should no longer be children, tossed to
and fro and carried about with every wind of
doctrine, by the trickery of men, in the cunning
craftiness of deceitful plotting;*

~ Ephesians 4:14

Chapter 10 – The Signs of Deception

The Signs of Deception

There are very clear signs of deception, and you can tick them off if you have the Dreams and Visions Workbook. Every dream that you receive and interpretation that you do, write it down and put it next to these points. And if it has any of these points in it, I want you to be very wary of that dream, because it is entirely possible that it was not sent of the Spirit of the Lord, but was sent by the enemy to discourage and deceive you.

Against the Word

The very first sign that a dream and revelation is not of the Lord is that it does not line up with the Word of God. That one is pretty clear. Anything that cuts against the Word of the Lord and the gospel of our testimony is not of the Spirit, or anything that turns man's attention away from the Lord. Jeremiah was given a word to the prophets of that time, in which he said, "You are turning the eyes of the people away from the living God and towards the things you would have them see and believe. You're making them follow you and man, instead of the Lord."

Be very wary of anything that distracts your attention away from the Lord and His work, because the Word says, "I will draw all men unto Me," not chase them elsewhere.

There was one revelation that was submitted to us at one time where the person in question had seen himself in vision, chained and working hard in the sun. He was being made to work hard, almost to death and his muscles ached with the agony. The interpretation that was offered along with this vision astounded me. The interpretation offered was that the Lord has put this person in bondage for a season for His own good will and purpose. That the Lord had to imprison him for his own good, so that he could be used of the Lord. And even though the work he did nearly killed him, it was for the Lords pleasure!

You only need to page through the Word of God to discover that the Lord is the one who frees us from our chains – not binds us in them! The Word says that His yoke is easy and His burden is light. He does not work us to death! Had this person just taken the time to apply their interpretation to the Word, they would have seen how they had fallen into deception by misinterpretation.

Fear

A very big indication is anything that produces fear. Any dream where you wake up and fear has gripped your heart uncontrollably, is not of the Spirit of God. Why? Because the Spirit of God is love. God is love and the opposite is fear. How do know that? Because the Scriptures say that, *'perfect love casts out fear.'* Any dream that has on it the taint of fear that grips you so that when you wake up the hair is still standing on the back of your neck, like we read in the passage of Job, is not of the Spirit of God. It is a deception, it is a lie from the enemy and you can throw that dream out. Tell Satan to take his lies where they belong and you reject it in the name of Jesus right away.

God does not promote fear. There is such a thing as the reverential fear of the Lord. But the kind of fear that is being spoken of here is not the reverential fear of the Lord. This fear causes the hair to stand up on the back of your neck; it causes you to tremble and become paralyzed; it causes you to look around to see if there is somebody in the room with you. You know the kind of fear I am talking of. I am sure that everybody in this world has had at least one nightmare where they wake up and the hair is standing on their head, and they feel that awful feeling all around them, like the room is closing in on them. This is not from the Spirit of God.

I have had occasions where people have submitted dreams and said, "I dreamt that my mother died. I dreamt that my sister was in a car accident. I dreamt that my child drowned. And when I woke up I had such fear in me. What must I do? Is the Lord warning me?"

No. The Lord is not warning you! Satan is trying to overtake your heart, your mind and your spirit with fear. And he knows that the minute you open that door to fear, he has access to your life. That is why he attacks you with fear, because fear is the very opposite of the nature of God. He knows that if you can open your heart with fear he has an entrance into your life.

If you are experiencing a curse in your life; if you are experiencing theft, strife, destruction and fear, then Satan has a foothold in your life. And nine times out of ten, it was fear that opened that door to him. If you can backtrack to when your heart was gripped in fear, when your heart skipped a beat – you opened a door and you gave a license to him by entertaining that thought for just a second. You close that door, tell Satan to go back where he came from, and you submit yourself to the Lord. You do not want to accept anything that is not of the Spirit of God, because the Spirit of God builds up, matures and encourages, and sets you on the right path.

There are times when there are messages in your dreams, and if you would identify them as the internal dreams they are you would have a better understanding of what is going on. I will post a dream here of death that had a totally different interpretation to what the person in question had in mind.

Example Dream:

"My daughter called me today. She is very distressed about a dream that she had last night. She said that it was very plain and vivid. Her brother, who is 22 and certainly lives on the wild side of life, was in this dream. She said that she was with him and he got shot in the head and the stomach. She said that she went to him and put his head in her lap and saw his face very plainly and a lot of blood. He told her that it was going to be all right, and she said she watched his face turn completely white, and he died. She then woke up and cried uncontrollably for 2 hours. What should I tell her?"

My Interpretation:

Firstly tell her that the dream is clearly internal and speaks of herself. Her brother speaks of the flesh in her dream. There is a part of her flesh that is being brought to death. It would seem, through the brutality of the dream, that this death will be a messy one.

In fact it is likely to be a leg-breaking experience for her. Has there been a direction she has been kicking against? Has she been going through pressures and not letting it go? If this is the case, then let her know that there is an issue the Lord is dealing with in her and that she needs to give it up to Him. This dream is indeed a warning one - but for her, not for her brother!

The Lord is making it very clear that unless she lets go and submits to the cross in her life, she will face a leg breaking and it will not be very easy for her. Teach her to 'Die already!' ok? I would also like to suggest that she close any doors to fear that she might have opened by misunderstanding the meaning of this dream. We certainly do not want Satan to have a foothold!

I trust this has helped ease your fears a bit and given some direction

Fear vs. Warning Dreams

If the Lord should give you a warning dream, particularly if you are in the prophetic ministry, it would not be tainted with fear. In fact, you will stop and wonder if the dream is perhaps symbolic and internal. I know this was the case when my dad had a dream that his father died. He woke up quite perplexed, because he did not have fear, but yet he could not put a symbol to his dream. He immediately thought it was internal and was confused as to what the dream may mean as he could not put symbols to the characters.

As it turned out, his father did go to be with the Lord a little while later. The Lord was giving him insight as a precursor of what was going to occur, but he did not wake up with that fear that grips you. He did not wake up with the fear and heavy oppression. Can you see the difference?

If there is one gift that I would pray to the Lord that every believer could have, it would be the gift of discerning of spirits. Because if every believer could sense what was from the Lord and what was from the enemy, they would constantly walk in victory. They would not take what the enemy is giving to them and eat it. Yet that is what is happening. The enemy has been feeding you a plate of lies and a bill of goods, but because you do not know the truth and the truth has not set you free, you have eaten it and consumed it. You have allowed it to enter your heart, it has gotten a hold of you, and now you cannot break free.

The light will dispel the darkness, and the sword of the Word will break that oppression that the enemy has put on you. Right now, if this is what you have been struggling with, particularly fear, I want you to stop and look at every entry point that you have given the enemy. And I want you to close that door and allow the Spirit of God to come and bring His love that will overcome every fear.

Guilt and Condemnation

The next sign that a dream is not of the Lord, is one that brings guilt and condemnation. Who is the accuser of the brethren? The Word of God says Satan is the accuser of the brethren. Even Jesus said that the enemy could not find any accusation in Him. There is no accusation in Jesus Christ. He came to give. He came to die. He came to give His very flesh and blood for you. Where would He stand up and accuse you and drive you into the dirt?

It is like the dream in Job that we read earlier, where this form appeared to Job in a dream and said, "Why do you think you're so special, when God Himself doesn't even give grace to His angels and doesn't even look after His servants? Who do you think you are to pray to God?"

Does this sound familiar? "Has God said?" Was that not said in Genesis by a certain serpent deceiving Eve? "Has God said?" It was questioning the Word of God and bringing accusation; bringing accusation to the Word of God and accusation to you.

Let me tell you, when the Holy Spirit convicts you, you will know, because you will fall onto your knees and you will weep before God. And you will say, "I am so unworthy of Your grace, and of Your honor and mercy," and your heart will be changed.

> *"For godly sorrow produces repentance leading to salvation, not to be regretted; but the sorrow of the world produces death." ~ 2 Corinthians 7:10*

Worldly sorrow produces death. It destroys you. It discourages you and it puts you into the ground. Any revelation that you receive externally or internally from dreams or any other gift of revelation that brings death upon you, is not the Spirit of God, because godly sorrow produces repentance to salvation never ever to be regretted of! There is no regret in you, because you come before the Lord with His blood and say, "I am cleansed by Calvary. I am cleansed by the Lamb." You are cleansed and conviction comes into your heart. And after you give that to the Lord, He makes you white as snow and there is no regret. There is joy and there is rejoicing, because that cloak of heaviness that you have been wearing for so long is stripped away.

A lovely example in the Word is of King Abimelech, as we shared in the first chapter, where he was guilty of taking Sarah, Abraham's wife into his harem. He fell on his knees and he said, "Lord, help me out here. I really didn't mean to do this." He was convicted. And what happened? The Lord sent Abraham to heal Abimelech and his people. It was repentance, not to be regretted of, because the Lord brought his healing. It was true conviction. It motivated him to action.

Satan the Accuser

Any accusation and condemnation that demobilizes you and makes you come to a standstill, is not the Spirit of God. If the Spirit of God is going to give you revelation He will give it to you so that you may apply it actively to your life. So if you are demotivated to the point where you have come to a standstill in your spiritual walk, you need to stop right there. I also want to state right now that I do not care if you have sinned; Satan has no right to accuse you. The Lord will stand judge.

I love reading through the story of Moses, because you know he made some terrible mistakes. But did you notice that God always vindicated him, even if Moses was in the wrong? God always vindicated him, because he stood on the Lord's side. It does not mean that because you have truly failed in your life and have sinned, that Satan has a right to accuse you and that you have a right to accept that accusation. The minute a sin is revealed to you, go and put it under the Blood and the Blood of the Lamb will cleanse you. And if something is brought up that you have taken to the cross before, it stays at the cross. You do not have to pick that burden up again.

Satan often comes with his accusation. Perhaps what he will do is give you dreams of your sin and a past event in which you failed the Lord or failed your family, and he will bring it back to your mind over and over again. This is not the Spirit of the Lord. This is Satan, sent to accuse and condemn you and to bring you down and discourage you. You reject it, in the name of Jesus, and you tell that accuser of the brethren where to put himself, because you will not listen to his lies any longer.

Forceful and Pushy

Another sign that a dream or revelation is a deception is that it is forceful. It compels you and pushes you. The Lord Jesus said that He was the shepherd. His sheep know His voice and He knows every one of them. A shepherd walks ahead of the sheep, and the sheep know and love his voice and they follow him. The shepherd does not stand behind the sheep and beat it with a stick. Anything that does not woo you, but instead condemns you and forces you, compelling you to action, is not of the Spirit of God.

Any revelation that insists that "You must get up and do this now!" and forces its will over your will, is not from the Lord. The Lord Jesus is a gentleman. He will not force His will over your will, and He will not force Himself on you. So anything that forces its will over your will, particularly if you have received a prior word that opposes this. Be very wary of before you jump up and respond to that word. Anything that compels you to action immediately, before you take that first step, stop! If it is not from the Lord, that impulse will eventually fade away.

God's Spirit is Gentle

If it is the Spirit of God though, it will continually nudge at you gently, and woo you, and encourage you in the right direction. If you have been struggling with a bad habit or something, the Lord will not rise up and say, "I demand that you give this up right now! I demand that you stop doing this in your life! I demand..." No. The Lord will always woo you in love. And when you are in love with somebody you will give up anything for them.

He will likely say, "You know what? When you do this, it really hurts Me. You know what? I'd be so blessed and encouraged if you would just give this thing up for Me."

That is the voice of your Savior. That is the voice of the Holy Spirit. He is likened to a dove. Since when does a dove fly on top of somebody's head and peck them to death? A dove is gentle, and if you are too rough with it, it will fly away. The Holy Spirit is a dove, and He will woo you to action. He will not demand and compel and insist, and peck, peck, peck at you. That is not how the Lord works, and it is not the Spirit that He operates in. Those are the different points to look out for, for deception.

Satanic Attack in Dreams

No weapon formed against you shall prosper, and every tongue which rises against you in judgment you shall condemn. This is the heritage of the servants of the Lord, and their righteousness is from Me, Says the Lord.

~ Isaiah 54:17

Chapter 11 – Satanic Attack in Dreams

I want to go on now, and discuss in particular how Satan attacks in our dreams. These dreams do not have any interpretation whatsoever. They are clearly an attack from the enemy in your sleep. They are pure nightmares in which demons appear in your dreams; in which you are fighting demons and demons are fighting you, or you are dying or drowning or something to that effect. Those are the kind of dreams where wake up and the hair is standing up on the back of your neck and you feel that presence in your room; that familiar presence of fear. And you know that Satan has attacked you in your sleep.

I cover in the *Prophetic Warrior Book* and *the Stain of Sin - Overcoming Curses* message, how to overcome the enemy in his attacks. I would recommend that you go and listen to, or read these materials. It is a foundational principle of everything that we share in our teachings. Satan actually has no right whatsoever over you, because of the Blood of Christ. He has no hold on you. Satan cannot just walk up to you at any time he pleases and pick on you. It is not the way it works. If Satan had the license to do that, he would have wiped out every believer by now. But he cannot, because he comes across the Blood, and he starts to cringe.

However, if Satan attacks you then he has license to attack you. If the enemy is attacking you in your sleep then there is an open door in your life and you are saying, "Here devil please come in. Would you a like a seat? Tea, coffee, juice?" He has gained entry. And if he has attacked you directly like that in your sleep, you are not a victim, you invited him. You need to determine how you invited him, and that is why I would like to encourage you to go and listen to or read that chapter, because it is too extensive for me to cover in detail here. I will however just touch on some of the points.

Contaminated Objects

Perhaps it could be that you have brought something, an object perhaps, into your home that has been contaminated. Just like Achan in the days of Joshua, when they went and defeated Jericho and he brought those objects into the tents of Israel. What happened is that Israel was suddenly defeated by their enemies. They cried out and said, "Lord, why?" And the Lord showed them that they had brought cursed objects into their camp, and it caused Satan to defeat them. Even so, you may have brought an object into your home, and it may have caused you to open the door to the enemy.

One example of this is of a couple who came to me, and their child was continually having nightmares. They had prayed with her, they had stood with her, and nothing they did stopped these nightmares, until they asked somebody to come and pray with them. And they saw, above the bed, a wall hanging. The minister kept being drawn to this wall hanging.

He said, "Where did you receive that from?"

It turned out that a foreign couple had given it to the child as a gift. If I am not mistaken I believe it was a Chinese wall hanging. But the point was, it was contaminated. It had been prayed over Satanically, and they had now brought this object into the child's room and placed it above her bed and this poor child could not sleep. She was having nightmares continuously. Obviously she was having nightmares continuously! They had invited Satan right into her bedroom and hung him over her bed! They simply prayed over the hanging and dedicated it to the Lord, and the nightmares stopped.

I have even had occasions with my own children, where I have brought things into their room, gifts sometimes that people have given, even sometimes magazines that have not had the Spirit of the Lord on them. I put it in their room and they have a spirit of restlessness in them and they come to us in the middle of the night with nightmares. When I go to investigate where Satan has gotten a hold, most of the time something has been put in their room that has been contaminated; an object.

Through People

Contamination and license can also come from your association with people that are not walking in the blessing of the Lord. They carry a curse within them. Perhaps they have been involved in the occult. Perhaps they are just believers that have gotten involved in things that they should not be getting involved in, and they carry on them that spirit of deception and divination. As you make contact with this person, your spirits connect, you pick up a contamination, and you carry it home with you. You open the door and let Satan right in. That night as you are going to sleep you are attacked time and time again.

I know, I have had this happen to me on many occasions, where I come across false prophets and come into confrontation with them, and I have very irresponsibly, forgotten to break the links with them. That night I cannot sleep for the nightmares that are assailing me. The minute I close my eyes, Satan uses that opportunity to attack me in my sleep. Such a coward, the enemy is. All I do is I wake up, break the links, and I tell Satan to get. It is really that simple.

The curses could be passed down from generations or from associations. Like I said, I am not going to cover it in detail. But if you are being attacked by demons in your sleep on a continual basis, Satan has an inroad. He has been given license. I would recommend you look around your room, see what you have brought into the room or into your home, and ask the Spirit of the Lord to open your eyes to where Satan has gained this hold on your life.

Practicalities

In conclusion, I would like you to take the dreams that you have written out, and I am going to go through that dream with you bit by bit now and show you how to identify whether it is a deception or not. Then I am going to show you how to identify, yet again, if it internal, healing, purging or garbage. This is the practical part of the chapter, so you can pull out your Workbook, pen and paper, and you can begin agreeing or disagreeing with the points that I am covering...

Deceptive Dreams

The very first thing... I want you to discard this dream as not of the Lord, if it has any of the following points:

- ✓ Firstly, discard the dream if you wake up with that spirit of fear attacking you, where you feel like the room is closing in on you, where you feel paralyzed. This dream was not of God.

- ✓ If you feel condemned; if you are not immediately moved to conviction and weep before the Lord and give Him this matter, but are feeling pushed once again into paralysis and depression, this was not the Spirit of God. Disregard this revelation.

- ✓ If you wake feeling accused, where lies are coming up in your head over and over again like, "Did you know you did this? And then you did that? And then you did this? Then you lied to this person and you treated this person like that. You did this sin, and you did that sin." That is not from the Lord. The Spirit of God brings conviction, in which you repent and are motivated to action. You are not discouraged to paralysis.

✓ If you feel compelled strongly to act on the dream immediately, this dream is not of the Lord, because the Spirit of God does not push. You feel like you are pushed from behind, from outside, like there is a pressure upon you to perhaps conform, to 'do'. Where something says in your dream, "Rise up and do it now. Act now, now, now!" This is not the Lord and I would submit this revelation to somebody who has a bit more experience in dream interpretation to sense the spirit on it if you are not quite able to do so yourself.

Now, you have identified whether the dream was a deception or not. If it is a deception, tear it up, throw it away and tell Satan to take his lies and get out. If you have opened a door to the enemy close it, but do not entertain the thoughts of that revelation any longer. Do not allow it to sow its seed of doubt, fear and condemnation.

The following is an example of such a dream. I would like you to note the points I just mentioned above in this dream:

Dream: Lady in Black

"In this dream there was a woman dressed in black from head to foot, including wearing a black veil over her face. Every time I watched myself talking to my husband he could not seem to hear me. However, whenever this woman in black spoke to him she would only whisper in his ears and he would respond by pointing his finger at me.

The next thing I was inside the dream, in a courtroom standing beside my husband and facing a judge. The same woman in black was standing on the other side of him. The judge told me that they had come to an arrangement about our three sons and that they were going to my husband. My husband only spoke up when this woman in black whispered in his ears. Again, the judge did not seem to hear me when I spoke. This is what the judge said to me. "You can see your children every four days and every fourth weekend." I remembered crying and crying. We walked out of the courtroom while this woman in black continued to walk on the other side of my husband.

Suddenly, I was outside of the dream watching myself. I was in our living room sitting on the settee opposite my mother who was asking me how it happened that my husband got the children. My mother then repeated the very same sentence the judge had spoken to me earlier "four days and every fourth month". Then in the dream I watched myself take two glasses and a bottle of wine. I placed the bottle on the floor near my feet. Just as I did this my husband burst into the room with the same woman in black at his side. He shouted at me, "Yes that is it! You are an alcoholic. That's right, that is what you are." I woke up.

In reality I am not an alcoholic, nor have I ever been. It is a known truth that I adore my children with a passion. Our marriage is good and we are not at all divided."

(**NOTE:** Your first reaction would be to look up the symbols and try to interpret this dream. It looks so like a straightforward internal dream, but if you would apply the principles I stated, you will see the deception in it. To try and interpret such a dream would lead you further into deception. Also note that the negative emphasis in this dream does not line up with the real relationship she has with her husband.)

My Interpretation:

"Upon reading your dream, something did not sit right on my spirit. Upon further study of your dream I noted something that I would like you to see. (Please note the principles here that I have written on deception. I would like you to see for yourself, what I have sensed here.)

I sensed all of these elements in your dream. There was fear, there was a lot of accusation and I also sensed that 'forcefulness'. This dream is a false revelation from the enemy and I would like to suggest that you close the door to any inroad you may have given Satan. There is no interpretation as it is a clear deception, so please reject it entirely."

Her response confirmed what I sensed.

Response:

God bless you and thank you Colette for such a speedy response. I actually woke up feeling the following:

Paralyzed into not pressing on with the things of the God.

Condemnation did set in and doubts about unworthiness and it was easier to for me to be quiet. If my voice was heard, then I will be discredited and shamed.

Yes, I did feel the pressure to conform to a superficial relationship with the Lord.

Emotions

Now that you have read your dream through and are sure it is not a deception, the first thing I want you to jot down is the emotion of the dream. How did you feel? Did you feel victorious? Did you feel fearful? Did you feel jealous? Did you feel strong? Did you feel insecure? Once you have determined the emotion of the dream, it actually gives you a very good path to run on, because now you know the emphasis. You know whether the emphasis is going to be one of needing healing, or an emphasis of one where you are already victorious and moving into something wonderful that the Lord has for you.

Look at the emotion of your dream. Was it healing? Did you wake up having faced a situation that you were victorious over? Not all negative emotions denote a negative dream, so do not see jealousy and anger as specifically negative dreams. It could be that you are a very quiet person, and in your dream you rise up in anger and act against a situation. This could very well be the Spirit of the Lord encouraging you to stand up and express yourself.

Even the Word says that God is a jealous God. Jealousy is not a sin. It is a natural, human emotion. Anger is not a sin, for the Word says, *"Be angry, but do not sin."* Anger is meant to motivate you to positive action, as is jealousy.

So do not see the emotions of the dream as necessarily a negative influence, because the Lord might be trying to get a message across to you that says, "Perhaps you need more of this emotion in your life." Or perhaps, "You need less of this emotion in your life." Or even perhaps, "This is where I'm leading you. You need to be more angry. You need to be angry for Me. You need to have righteous indignation. You need to be jealous over My people. I want you to be jealous over My people!"

Can you see how identifying the emotion of a dream gives you a very good track to run on? You need to determine if it is negative or positive. Your emotions will pretty much give you a track to run on. Ask yourself, "Did I wake up feeling as if something was amiss in my spirit? There is perhaps something negative in my life that needs to be dealt with."

I am not talking about condemnation. I am talking about that deep stirring inside that says, "I need to deal with this area of my life." Or, "I've gone off the path that the Lord has had me on. I need to get back on it."

If you are dreaming that you are driving along in your car and suddenly your car goes off the road, this has a negative connotation, in which it could be saying, "You were on the right track, but you're being sidetracked. You need to get back onto the path again." Or perhaps you have been dreaming that you have been driving on the side of the road and suddenly you turn off onto a main highway. This dream would have a very positive connotation in that it is saying, "You were off the track, but you are on the right track again."

Of course, I am referring here specifically to internal dreams. Identify whether it is something negative in your life that needs to be fixed, or something positive that the Lord is motivating you towards.

What Type of Dream?

Now identify if your dream is healing, purging, garbage or prophetic.

Healing Dreams

In your dream, did you perhaps dream of past events that you were victorious over? Did you perhaps dream of characters from the past, friends from the past, teachers of the past, even buildings of the past? Were there smells that you were familiar with from the past; colors that represented something from the past? Anything that perhaps relates to childhood and adolescence, but in the dream you had victory.

Perhaps you have had a bad relationship with your mother, but in your dream, you and her are embracing and a bond is formed. This is a healing dream. This is the Lord taking away the hurt and anguish that has been in you, and He is just saying, "I'm healing this area of your life. You won't need to worry about it anymore." If that is the case, if you are dreaming about circumstances that are very familiar to you and you are having victory, it is a healing dream, in which case it has no clear interpretation other than it is just the Lord confirming His work in your life.

Purging Dreams

Perhaps you are dreaming that you are giving into temptation. This would be your purging dream, in which your subconscious is simply letting out in your mind all those stimuli which you have been feeding into it during the day. Perhaps you got mad at your boss and you really felt like hitting him, and in your dream you are actually beating the stuffing out of him. This would simply indicate a purging dream. It does not have an interpretation other than it was just your inner man living out your fears, temptations and ambitions in your dream.

Perhaps you are dreaming that you have won the lottery, or maybe you are dreaming that you are laying your hands on people and they are just falling under the power. This is not necessarily a prophetic dream. It could very simply be the desires of your heart. It is just a purging dream, and your subconscious is throwing out all those inner desires and conflicts and everything that you have been feeding in.

I know I have had many people submit dreams in which they are saying, "I was standing in front of this huge congregation. I went along the healing line, and every single person was healed and fell under the power."

It is a great dream and it could even be the Lord confirming the call on a person's life, but that is not necessarily a prophetic word, other than simply the desire of the person's heart. If somebody has a keen desire for evangelism they could dream that they are evangelizing the nations. That is not necessarily prophetic. It could simply be their inner desires that are being displayed in their dreams. So it is very important to get the background information of the person whose dream you are interpreting, so you can place the dream in the context where it belongs.

Garbage Dreams

Garbage dreams are very clear to identify. Those are your movie dreams. Those are when you say; "If I could have put that dream into a script it would have been a billion dollar production." It is one of those dreams, where you are dreaming of aliens and space ships, and models and who knows what else. There are many different scene changes one after the other with complicated characters in them. It is a very complex dream with a lot of detail and stimuli, a lot of feelings, a lot of changes and a lot of activity.

This is very clearly a garbage dream. I have had people come to me with dreams that are six pages long and they say, "I gave this dream to you in detail. What is its interpretation? It was so clear. It must have an interpretation."

It had scene change after scene change. They went to town, then they were at home, then they were in the basement, and then they were on the roof. Then this person came to them and said this, and then another person came and said, "No, what that person's saying is not right." Then they were speaking to this person, and then... It is a garbage dream.

The Spirit of God is not a God of confusion, and if He gives you revelation, He will not mince His words and He will not contradict Himself. He will give you a very clear and simple word. A dream with many scene changes, that is overcomplicated, and that usually went through the entire evening of your sleep is just your mind throwing out the garbage that you have been feeding into it since the day you were born.

Prophetic Dreams

As you know, there are three types of prophetic dreams. In this dream, were you the star character? If you can say 'yes', tick it off, it is internal. If 'no', if you were standing out on the outside looking in, it was an external prophetic dream.

Was the dream very simple? A dream that is from the Holy Spirit will be very simple. And it is entirely possible that you will have three quick dreams one after the other, all with the same message, just as in the days of Joseph where Pharaoh dreamt of the seven cows and then of the seven ears of wheat. They were two very quick dreams with the same emphasis and message. So if the Lord is really trying to get something across to you, usually prophetically, He will give you a couple of dreams or visions, one after the other, that all have the same emphasis, the same emotion and sometimes even the same numbers or colors. Perhaps something specific will stand out in the dream. In the case of Pharaoh the number seven was specific in his dream, and the lean and the fat.

So, if you have had a few quick dreams, and all of them are clear, pick out the symbols in each dream that were very prominent and write them down. The internal prophetic dream will also be very clear, but it usually pertains to your ministry or future events. It does not pertain to your current spiritual condition, as does the straight internal dream.

Perhaps in your dream you have a key and you are opening a door. The Lord could very well be saying, "I am going to be leading you into the prophetic. You will

be using what I have given you on behalf of others."
That could be an internal prophetic dream.

Perhaps you dream of a situation of where you are in a
church, an old-style building, you are leaving and it is
being burnt behind you. The Lord is saying, "I'm taking
you out of that religious mindset. You are going to be
moving on."

Perhaps you are dreaming of putting coffins in the
ground, or of dead bodies. This could very well be an
internal dream, or even a prophetic dream where the
Lord is saying, "There is a part of your flesh that needs to
die, and you won't let it die. Let it go!"

Next time we are going to go into characters and
symbols and you will be able to pull out the pieces and
begin to interpret your dreams and visions piece by
piece. But firstly I want you to understand how to
identify the emotion and then to identify what type of
dream it is, before you begin the actual interpretation of
symbols. It is no use trying to interpret a dream that has
no interpretation. It is no use taking a demonic
revelation and trying to interpret it by the Spirit of God.
It does not work. It is no use taking a dream that is just
simply your mind throwing out garbage and trying to
interpret it, as you will confuse yourself and you will go
on to confuse others too. And you are going to end up in
hot water, because people are not going to be
impressed.

External Prophetic Dreams

In the external prophetic dream, obviously this is where you are standing out looking in. Once again, it is a very clear dream. It is not overcomplicated, but it does tend to have a bit more detail and the symbols will be very clear. You will see specific characters and symbols that will be very clear as to what they represent.

It has a future orientation. The external prophetic dream operates as the word of wisdom in that it has a future orientation. Another good way to identify if a dream is externally prophetic is that the characters that you usually use in your internal dreams cannot be interpreted. The symbols are common to you. You see, the Holy Spirit will always bring up from your spirit and mind, symbols that are common to you. As we discussed in King Nebuchadnezzar's dream, the Lord used an illustration of an idol; a big statue with its head of gold and so on. The Lord will use symbols that are very common in your internal dreams, so that you can understand His message.

You will dream of people that you are familiar with, and so from that familiarity you can identify what they symbolize. In an external dream the symbols and characters in your dream are not of the usual sort. They are perhaps people you have never met before, and they are perhaps symbols that you have never had in your dreams before. But like I said, the external dream is specifically geared towards the Prophetic Ministry. So if you have been having those kinds of dreams, it could be that the Lord is leading you into that Office.

Next time we will take a look at characters and people in your dreams; how to look at them, analyze your relationships with them, and determine what they mean in your dreams. And so you are going to discover that they are used often for a reason, because the Holy Spirit is trying to use them to get a message across to you. And it will be very exciting next time as you start looking at the practical application.

But for now, I want you to take this chapter and I want you to apply it to your life. I want you to stand against any deception that Satan might have put in you, and to put it aside. Do not dwell on it. Do not allow yourself to be discouraged. Simply deal with the open door and put it away. Then open your heart to the Spirit of the Lord and say, "Lord, I am here. Speak to me."

CHAPTER 12

Interpreting Symbols in Dreams and Visions

13 These things we also speak, not in words which man's wisdom teaches but which the Holy Spirit teaches, comparing spiritual things with spiritual.

14 But the natural man does not receive the things of the Spirit of God, for they are foolishness to him; nor can he know them, because they are spiritually discerned.

~ 1 Corinthians 2:13-14

Chapter 12 – Interpreting Symbols in Dreams and Visions

Wisdom Needed

Finally, we come to the most practical chapter in this entire series of The Way of Dreams and Visions. It is the chapter you have been waiting for and hoping I would finally get round to, and here it is! I would like to open with a passage that I believe should be the key passage for this chapter concerning interpreting dreams and visions by the Spirit of God. The reading is from 1 Corinthians 2:13-14

> *"These things we also speak, not in words which man's wisdom teaches but which the Holy Spirit teaches, comparing spiritual things with spiritual.*
>
> *But the natural man does not receive the things of the Spirit of God, for they are foolishness to him; nor can he know them, because they are spiritually discerned."*

As I go through some of the common symbols and characters in this chapter, I would like you to keep this passage in mind, because without the wisdom and the Spirit of God, you will not be able to interpret your dreams or visions correctly. The world has tried it. They have given you 'ten easy steps' on how to interpret your dreams and visions.

The Spirit of the Lord is not like the wisdom of man. It comes by revelation and it comes supernaturally. This should always be your motivation when interpreting dreams and visions. What is the Lord trying to say? What is the message from the Word of God? This should always be your emphasis - to reach out for yourself to touch the wisdom of the Lord. Each and every one of us need to be looking to the Lord for revelation. If every member in the Body of Christ received revelation from the Lord, they would be able to interpret the will of the Lord in their own lives.

Unique to You

So many of the things I will be sharing with you here are not etched in stone. They are not carved and set as a rule for every single person, because every person is an individual in their feelings, in their opinions, in their templates and in the way they have been brought up. So you cannot take one set of circumstances and superimpose it on the life of another person, because the two will not match.

The Lord has created each and every one of us uniquely. There is not a single organ or member of the body that is absolutely identical to the other. Even your two little fingers are not identical. Your one ear is bigger than the other one. Your one eye is bigger than the other one. When coming to receive revelation for yourself, realize that what worked for your brother or sister is not going to work for you, because the Lord has a message for you specifically. So as you start tapping into the wisdom of the Spirit and seeing those familiar symbols appear in your life personally time and time again, you will start seeing a blueprint forming. You will then be able to take that blueprint and apply it to further revelations that you receive personally from the Spirit of the Lord.

So as I share I would like you to see types. I would like you to see shadows. I would like you to see symbols that are common to your own life. I do not want you to look around and compare yourself to others. I want you to look at your life. I want you to see how these symbols relate to you; how they appear to you; how you see them and view them; how you can personally identify. Then as you learn to identify those symbols in your own life you will then be able to reach out and help others identify it in their lives. But until you have experienced it for yourself and until you know yourself how it works, you will not be able to reach out and help others receive the revelation for themselves.

Symbols in Visions

We have discussed over the course of the last three chapters, the difference between the internal and the external prophetic revelations that we receive in dreams and visions.

Prophetic Symbols Constant

Now, when it comes to the prophetic symbols it is very easy for me to pull out many Scriptures to back up what I am saying, because the Lord, when speaking prophetically, will never double-cross Himself. He will always speak the same. He is not the God of confusion; He is the God of order. When He speaks prophetically through one person, He will speak prophetically through another person in the same way. His revelations will all line up and tie up with the Word of God, because the Word of God is our standard. It is what we use as a guideline in the spiritual realm. So in the prophetic realm, everything relates to the Word of God, and we can see the symbols, types and shadows from the Word.

Internal Symbols Change

However, when it comes to internal revelation via dreams and visions, this is where the change occurs, because when we are discussing internal revelation we are speaking revelation from your own spirit. It is revelation that is coming up from your own templates in life.

Now, your templates are not the same as the templates of the guy next to you, so your internal dream will pertain entirely to your circumstance, whereas his internal dream will pertain to him. You could both have the same prophetic visions, but when it comes to internal dreams and visions they are for you and you alone.

These internal dreams are always based on the templates of life. Why is that? It is because the revelation comes from your spirit into your mind. It is reflected through your templates. It will be reflected through your sex, through your race, through your culture, through your doctrinal stands and beliefs, through everything in fact that you have been brought up to believe. It will show in your moral code, the way you feel and the way you have reacted in life. Can you see now, why interpretation of dreams and visions can be so diverse? You just take a few of those points and you take a couple of people and look how they vary. In culture alone the symbols can vary drastically.

Internal Interpretations

So the first part I am going to look at is the influences of internal interpretation. By internal interpretation, I am talking about the interpretation that is specific to you from your spirit. This is the dream that operates as the word of knowledge. In other words it pertains to things, past and present, that are happening in your life right now or did happen in your life in the past.

Moral Codes

They are based on your templates. They could be based on your moral codes, on the way you have been brought up. Not everybody has been brought up with the same moral code. What you may have learned was wrong and right, somebody else may not have learned as they were growing up. It also pertains to culture. In some cultures things are acceptable. In other cultures things are not acceptable.

So if you are in a dream where perhaps you are doing something against the moral code that was built into you that would have a negative connotation, because it is a place of discomfort. It is a place where you are out of order. If you were always taught to be well-mannered and polite and that is a way of life, and in your dream you are being unruly and rebellious and out of order, it has a negative implication, because it goes against the grain. It goes against who you are and what you are.

There are other people in this world, however, who were born rude and unruly and obnoxious. I am sure you could give me a list of names. I myself could give you a list of names of people who do not seem to have any moral code in that area at all! So when they dream of being unruly, it would not be anything out of the ordinary for them. That would be something very plain and standard for them. Can you see the difference, just in moral codes?

Fears

Then there are fears. There are certain things that you as an individual will fear. Choose anything. You may be afraid of the dark. You may be afraid of certain animals, perhaps insects. Perhaps you had a bad experience as a child with fire or something like that and so you have grown up with this fear.

Let's take for example that you have a fear of spiders. Now, when you dream of such a symbol, what connotation do you think that spider would have? Think about that. It would represent your fears! Because spiders are something that you fear in your real life, when you dream of spiders, that spider would then be a representation of your inner fears that you have been carrying around your entire life. Each individual has their own unique fear. You would need to identify yours. Whatever the case, if you dreamed of a symbol that in real life you are truly afraid of, that symbol in your dream would be a representation of a spirit of fear.

Example of a Dream

A good illustration is a dream that somebody who was afraid of spiders shared with me. In her dream she had a box of spiders. She used to dream frequently of spiders, because they were her greatest fear. And when she dreamt of spiders, she knew that her spirit was saying, "This is your fear. This is a fear you're having to face."

In this dream she had a box with spiders in it. She looked at it and she came to terms with it and she calmed herself down. She could handle that. Then she put the spiders down and took the lid off the box and she could see them. They were close enough and she could handle it. Then suddenly the box was pushed across the floor and the spiders started pouring out of the box. At first she started handling it, but then suddenly she started getting to a point where she was panicking and she could not handle it anymore. Then she woke up.

The obvious and direct interpretation of that dream is this. There is something in this person's life that they fear, and they are being forced to face that fear head-on. They know they need to face it. They know that this is something that they have to confront in their lives, and they have been facing it, up to a point. They have been steadily making progress, but then suddenly things are happening and they are becoming overwhelmed, the fear is too much for them and they lose control.

In this case, this particular person had been led into a ministry that she felt inadequate to do at that time. She felt that it was over her head and she feared failure. Yet she entered into it and at first had good control of the situation and was handling the load. The interpretation indicated that even though she began to handle this task, that she was originally afraid of getting involved in, it had now got to the stage where the responsibilities had overcome her and had overwhelmed her again.

Can you see how the spiders were used as an illustration of fear? You see, such a picture does not necessarily have to be demonic. What a spider will mean to you is not what a spider will mean to somebody else in an internal dream. However in an external dream or vision, the spider has an entirely different interpretation, so once again I will reiterate how important it is that you identify the difference between an internal and an external dream.

Insecurities

Insecurities are a big template that is often played out in your dreams. Perhaps you are insecure about your physical features. Perhaps you are insecure about certain abilities. Now, if you are insecure about perhaps the way you speak, when you have a dream that you get up to speak and you make an absolute fool of yourself, all that is happening is that your inner fears are being revealed through that insecurity. But perhaps you have a dream where you stand up to speak and you are bold, eloquent and confident and you are well received. Suddenly that has a good connotation in your dream. It means a good thing. It builds you up and it is positive. These dreams are often recurring.

Passions and Desires

What about passions? What about things that you truly desire? Perhaps you have a desire to preach. Perhaps it is something that really burns in you, and it is a positive picture in you, but you dream something really negative about preaching. That would have a negative connotation because preaching is your desire and passion. It is a positive thing.

Perhaps you are standing up in front of an entire congregation and you are making a fool of yourself while you are trying to preach. Perhaps you are being accused, in which case it is a very good indication that you are coming under condemnation about those things that you are good at and those things that you are confident at, and it is an attack.

Can you see how your templates very much interfere with the revelations the Lord gives you internally? Dreaming out your inner desires, such as preaching, flying, acting, singing or any other ability you are not good at in the natural, will often be recurring as well.

Relationships

Then the most common symbols are those regarding relationships. This is a big one and you will also find your answers embedded in your templates.

Your Mother

What about dreaming of your mother? There could be a whole myriad of interpretations for this one. As an individual you need to assess where your relationship is at with your mother personally. What your mother will mean to you is not what it will mean to somebody else. You need to look at your own relationship with her, how you feel about her. Get down to basics. Do not try and kid yourself and pretend to be something you are not. Look at what you really feel about her.

If you have a negative impression of your mother, perhaps she is the kind of person who stands in your way. Perhaps she humiliates you. Perhaps she abused you as a child. In your dreams and visions she will not represent something that is positive. She could very easily represent the flesh; those things that Satan would use to accuse you, stumbling blocks, rocks in the road, things that would trip you up. She would not have been a good picture in your life. If you have a bad relationship with your mother she will not be a good representation in your dreams.

Perhaps you have had a good relationship with your mother; maybe she raised you up correctly and you have a good bond with her; she poured into you and you had a lot of respect for her. Then when you dream of your mother it could be a positive picture. Solomon speaks in Proverbs of how you should not forget the law that your mother poured into you.

Perhaps you are dreaming that your mother is helping you give birth to something. Very often, your mother could represent the church; those things that teach you and feed you and birth things in you. But you need to assess if it is positive, or if it is negative? It is not carved in stone. It is to your specific individuality.

An example of a dream that comes to mind is a dream where John (not his real name) dreamed that his mother had taken over the driving of his car. They were going through highways and byways at full speed. It was a crazy ride and yet they did not seem to be getting anywhere. Upon questioning the relationship that John had with his mother, it turned out that he and his mother were not on good terms. His mother was the kind of person that dominated him and tried to control his life. So in his dream, his mother represented his flesh.

This dream had a very clear interpretation: His flesh was in control of his ministry, and because of this he was getting nowhere! The advice was for him to search his heart and to get back into the Lord's will. To put that flesh on the cross and to walk in the Lord's divine will. This interpretation was confirmed as John had come to a plateau in his spiritual life and he realized that he had let the pressures of life allow him to resort to natural methods to control his ministry.

Your Father

What about a father figure? A father figure is usually the easiest if you have had a good relationship with him. A father figure very often, from my personal experience, represents the Lord, our Heavenly Father. Perhaps you are viewing your Heavenly Father the same way that you are viewing your earthly father, who may not have treated you so well.

Perhaps you did not have a very loving father and you felt distant, and you did not feel very loved. And now as you come to your Heavenly Father you feel the same way. Perhaps in your dreams you are dreaming that your father is still treating you the same way, and that hurt is still there. Perhaps the Lord is trying to get a message across to you that says, "Hey, I'm not the same way as your earthly father. Allow Me to reach in and help you with this one."

It is very often a picture of the Heavenly Father. But then again, if your father was abusive and destroyed your life, he may represent your fear, your insecurities. Once again the flesh will be portrayed.

I was given a dream to interpret by someone by the name of Mark (not his real name). He dreamed that he was trying to speak to his father on the phone and that he could not get through. In his dream he felt frustrated, and as much as he tried, he could not get through to speak to him. On questioning Mark I found out that his father was a very distant character in his life. Although his father did love him, he never expressed that love and so there was always this barrier between them.

The dream was indicating that Mark was seeing the Lord in the same way as he saw his natural father – unapproachable. He had come to a point in his spiritual life, where he seemed to hit a roof and could not get past it. This was lived out in his dream and the Lord was revealing that his misconceptions of his father were the very thing that were holding him back from entering into a relationship with his Heavenly Father. Mark gave the matter to the Lord and asked for forgiveness of past judgments of his father and he was set free to enter into the fullness of his call.

Spouse

What about your spouse – your husband or wife? Once again, assess the relationship with your spouse. I personally have come to find that if you have a positive relationship with your spouse, it very often represents our Heavenly Bridegroom, who is the Lord Jesus Christ. So when I dream that my husband is taking me somewhere or giving me a gift or trying to get a message across to me, I know that something with my relationship with the Lord Jesus is about to change and adapt.

If I dream that my husband puts me in the car and is taking me somewhere, I know instinctively that what my spirit is saying to me is that the Lord wants to take me to another level in my ministry. He wants to take me to another place in our relationship.

If I dream that I am estranged from my husband, that perhaps we have been separated somehow, my ears prick up. I think, "Uh oh, something has happened to my personal relationship with the Lord Jesus. I need to find out what's happened."

You see, as you begin identifying these symbols one by one, you will start forming those pictures, and the next time you have those dreams they will seem so much clearer to you and you will pick up the revelation much easier.

Siblings

What about siblings? Well, this one can be a bit tricky. I do not know if siblings very often have a positive connotation, because they are the ones who picked on you. They are the ones who gave you a tough time. If you have a bad relationship with them and there was competition as you grew up, your siblings could very well be a representation of your bitterness. They could represent your jealousy. How you feel towards your sibling could actually be a representation of what they are in your dream.

So if you dream of your sibling rising up and taking over and they represent your bitterness, perhaps the Lord is saying, "Your bitterness is taking over your life. Bitterness is taking hold of you. You had better sort it out." If you dream that your sibling dies and they represent bitterness, then the dream would have a positive interpretation, meaning that the Lord has removed bitterness from your life.

However, you may have had a positive relationship with your siblings. Perhaps you had a big brother or sister that always took care of you and made sure that you were looked after. Perhaps they were always there for you to lean on and they were a fortress of protection. They could very well represent the Holy Spirit in your life and how He takes care of us, lifts us up and motivates us on to the next level.

Friends

Then there are your friends. What does dreaming of your friends speak of? You need to assess what kind of friends you are dreaming of. Personally I know that when I am dreaming of the friends that I had when I was in my little 'rebellious stage' in my teens, I know that I am dreaming about the past. I know that I am dreaming about rebellion. I know that I am dreaming about something that is not so positive, because they represented an entire era of my life where I was not in touch with the Lord, where I was out of order, where I was not walking the way I should have been.

So when I start dreaming that I am making contact with past friends or falling in love with old boyfriends who were in that bad scene, I prick up my ears, because then the Holy Spirit is saying to me, "Be careful. You're getting into the flesh. You're getting back into areas where you should not be getting into."

But you do have those friends that motivated you in the Lord. They supported you. They led you to the Lord. Perhaps they taught you everything they know about the Lord. They poured into you the Word, the Scriptures, time, counsel, and a lot of love as well. When you dream about that, it could also very well represent the Holy Spirit, those things that pour into you and give you revelation, enable you and build you up.

You need to discern what it is. Is it positive? Is it negative? What does this group of people represent? When you think of the person in your dream, when you think of them in the natural, what is the first impression that comes to you? That is what you need to think. What is that first impression? Because that first impression is what is going to last, and that first impression is what your inner man is going to use to try and portray the symbol in your dreams and in your visions.

Gender and Race in Dreams & Visions

And He has made from one blood every nation of men to dwell on all the face of the earth, and has determined their preappointed times and the boundaries of their dwellings;

~ Acts 17:26

Chapter 13 – Gender and Race in Dreams & Visions

Your gender is also very particular in dreams and visions, especially when they are internal. I dream or have visions of the Lord clothing me in beautiful bride's gowns and putting flowers in my hair. Now, my husband does not have the same kind of dream. If my husband had to dream that he was having flowers put in his hair, he would think, "What is going on? I'm missing it somewhere bad," because that is something so out of the ordinary. It is bad, it is negative and it is against who he is. It is like two identical poles of a magnet that cannot join.

Now, if I was dreaming that I was taking up the car tools and getting stuck into the engine of the car I would think, "What am I doing? That's a man's responsibility. That's a man's job."

I had a dream posted where a lady dreamt that she was wearing a man's shoes. Now, a woman does not wear a man's shoes. It is out of place. It is opposite to what you are and who you are in reality. So that would have an absolute negative connotation of, "You're doing something that you shouldn't be doing. You're walking a walk that you shouldn't be walking, because those are a man's shoes. A woman doesn't wear a man's shoes. It is out of place." But for a man to be walking around in man's shoes is really quite ordinary. However, if a man dreamt that he was walking around in high heels, he had better sit up and take notice, because something is wrong. He is walking the wrong walk.

Can you see how our templates are particular to our gender? And your inner man is going to use these. If you are dreaming something that is so alien to you and who you are, it is an absolute negative connotation. You are not where you should be. Something is wrong with this picture. It is not ordinary. It is not right. It is alien to you.

Example of a Dream

I was thinking of one example of a dream that my husband had where he dreamt that he and his dad went to go and watch a rugby match. It was a good, positive healing dream. Now for American's who do not know what rugby is, it is a sport very similar to football, but without all that protective gear. He and his dad were taken to this rugby match, and it was a wonderful atmosphere. There was joy and they were having a good time, and it was such a lovely picture of the relationship that he had started developing with his Heavenly Father. They were having a good time together. They were becoming buddies. They were bonding.

Now if I had dreamt the same thing, that my dad had taken me to a football match, I would sit up and take notice, because I do not even watch the sport! It is just not in my nature to even care. That is not my idea of bonding. But for a guy that is his idea of bonding, so the inner man will use that picture for him to put that message across. If I had to dream like that I would definitely think, "Something is wrong. Why am I dreaming this? I'm out of place. I shouldn't be in this kind of environment. Lord, where have I stepped out of line?" But for a man to dream something like that, it is perfectly in order and it is positive and builds him up.

The Anima and Animus

Have you ever noticed in your dreams that you sometimes have a male or female character with you? Perhaps you do not know who they are and you do not recognize them, but yet in your dream they are somebody that is very close to you. You do not know who they are and you do not recognize their facial features, but yet you are close and intimate with them. When you dream of those they very often represent your feminine (anima) and masculine (animus) nature.

Every one of us has a feminine and masculine side, and it is totally related to your right and left-brain thinking. A woman is naturally very allegorical. She is born with woman's intuition, as the common myth says. She is very picturesque. She thinks in pictures. Men, on the other hand, think very logically. They think very differently to women. This has been scientifically proven, so if you are a Woman's Libber do not jump in here and fight with me, okay?

Men think with a different kind of logic. They are more methodical and more intellectual in their thinking, whereas women can be more 'fluffy'. Men are not. Men like practical things. Let's be honest, when you are doing shopping for Christmas or birthday gifts, you get the woman the 'fluffy' stuff, and you get the man the practical stuff and that is what he is happy with. You can always buy a man tools and he is always happy, even if it is the same thing. You do not buy a woman pots, okay, for all you men reading this book! For a woman you buy things that are pretty and attractive and things that pamper her. It is the way we are. It is the way God has created us.

Each and every one of us have both an anima (feminine side) and an animus (masculine side). Even a woman can think very logically and intellectually, as well as thinking very allegorically. Now, a man can also think very much in pictures and yet also be intellectual. So when you dream of the male and female counterparts, these are the different symbols that they represent. If you are dreaming of this man that you are always becoming intimate with, then what is happening is your inner man is saying, "You're becoming more intellectual. You are moving more towards the teaching side. You've become more methodical in the way that you've been approaching life and the way that you've been approaching ministry."

In experience and in giving counsel in dream interpretation to a lot of the ministers that we train up, we have discovered that the masculine side very often represents a more teaching-oriented ministry, whereas the female often represents a more prophetic and allegorical type of ministry.

Personal Example

So when the Lord took me through a transition from prophet through to teacher I kept on having scandalous dreams. Every night I would dream that I was embracing this tall handsome man and I enjoyed it, but yet I knew I was married and I used to wake up with such guilt and condemnation. I thought, "My goodness! I haven't been watching TV and I haven't been reading books, so where is this coming from? There's something wrong with me."

It continued until I realized what it was. My spirit was saying very clearly, "You need to start embracing the teaching side of your ministry gifts. Put away the prophetic for now. Put away your feminine side and start moving to a more intellectual, methodical, logical and teaching way of thinking."

Perhaps you have been having strange dreams where you have been embracing this woman and you really enjoy it, and you wake up feeling bad and guilty that you are having an affair in your sleep. Perhaps the Spirit is trying to say, "Hey, you need to embrace more of your feminine side. You need to think a little bit more allegorically. Stop being so stuck in a rut. Stop being so methodical. Let it hang loose a bit and start becoming a little bit more feminine. Start thinking in pictures. Start thinking in symbols and in types and shadows, instead of always being so Word-based and so structured." Can you see the opposites?

Another Good Example

I was looking to the Lord for a dream that I could give you as an example for this, and just before this chapter came together, somebody shared a dream with me that lines up exactly with what I have been sharing, with regards to the female and male counterparts.

A lady had a dream, and in the dream she found herself coming to a flight of stairs. These were strange kinds of stairs, however. They were the kind of contraption that you have in amusement parks for their water rides, where you get in a cart and a chain pulls you in the cart up the stairs, then you go onto a landing and then go on to the slides… You know the kind of 'stairs' I am talking about?

She came to these stairs which were bright blue in color and there was water pouring over them. So she got into the cart at the bottom of the stairs and she was pulled up all the way to the top. As she came to the top landing she looked around and there were a whole lot of couples together. It was some kind of institution, some kind of gathering. But as she stood there she felt very insecure about herself. She felt out of place. She felt, "What am I doing here? I don't belong. Look at all these people. They have their place; they're comfortable and know each other. They know what they're doing, and here's me out of place."

She felt totally ill at ease as if she did not belong, so she tried to get out. She went to a landing opposite to the one she had been at, and as she came in, there were another group of people, but these people were all men and they were homosexual. The strange thing was, however, as she came to be amongst this group of homosexual men, she felt comfortable. She felt at ease. There were a group of men who were dancing and some of them had dressed up like women. She said they looked so much like real women. They were dancing and she was dancing with them and they accepted her. She felt so comfortable with it.

Then suddenly in her dream she got this eerie feeling that said, "Hang on a minute, what am I doing here?" Suddenly everything that had been so joyous went dull and went dark, and she could feel oppression. Suddenly the race was on to get out of there and there were strange things happening and it was haunted. There were men out to get her and so she ran out. As she left this building she came out and looked up and she saw a similar set of stairs, also blue, with the water coming down and the cart at the bottom. They looked like the same set of stairs, as the first, but in this case the stairs were crooked. They were not straight like they were in the first picture.

She ran away and returned to where she started. She went up the original set of stairs to the first place she went to where the groups of men and women were, and with a big sigh of relief she landed there and woke up.

Interpretation:

This is a very good dream for me to explain to you what I mean about the male and female counterparts. The stairs and the water very clearly speak of rising up in ministry, blue being a heavenly color. The water represents the anointing of the Spirit. She was going to rise up very quickly in ministry. As she got there, there were couples of men and women. The Lord was leading her into using both the teaching and the prophetic ministries. He was leading her into a promotion, but it was a new realm of ministry. As she got there, however, she felt uncomfortable and thought, "What am I doing here? These people know what they're doing. They're better than me, they're more mature than I am."

I am sure you can relate to this one. She felt, "I'm just little me. Nobody will listen to me. What am I even doing here? Why am I even trying to pretend to be something that I'm not" and so she left and went to the other group of gay men.

Now what happened in reality, is that this particular lady had been operating very well in the teaching arena. She had overdeveloped the masculine side of her character. She was very methodical in her thinking, very intellectual. Now the Lord was trying to push her more to the feminine side, but she was trying to hang on to the masculine side. What it represented was that she was trying to go in the direction that the Lord said she must. She was trying to flow prophetically, but she was doing it using her intellect and the old way of doing things. The men dressing up as women represented this emphasis. She was trying to pretend to be something that she was not. She was trying to use her intellect and her natural skills to flow prophetically, which you cannot do. You cannot mix the two.

So what the dream was saying was, "You'd better watch it, because you're going to get yourself into deception. If you keep on trying to figure this out with your intellect and with your mind, and if you keep on trying to flow as a prophet using your teaching abilities, you're going to end up getting into deception," which represented the crooked stairs and the whole situation turning eerie. The Lord was saying very clearly, "Get back to where you started and excel in the ministry I've given you, and I'll give you what you need. But don't try to use something in the natural and use your intellect."

So can you see the two pictures? If you have been dreaming of a male character being in your dreams all the time, perhaps you are being nudged towards a more teaching orientation. But if there is a woman in your dreams all the time, who you seem to know in your dream, but when you wake up you do not know her, she could very well represent your prophetic side and the Lord is nudging you towards that way of thinking.

Keep this in mind as you interpret your dreams and visions, because this one will crop up more than any of the other symbols that we have discussed so far. You will find that there is always a masculine or feminine character with you in your dream. Sometimes you cannot see them because they are standing behind you, but you may be aware of their presence. And when you are aware of their presence and you identify them in your dreams, you are going to know what I am talking about.

Your Race and Culture

You will also dream according to your race and culture. Now for me, being a white person, if I dream of a native person in my dreams it has a negative connotation for me, because they are not the same as me. They are opposite to me. I am not comfortable in my dream with that kind of thing. However, if you are a black person and you dream of a white or some other kind of race in your dream, they would represent something negative to you, because they are alien to your natural birth culture. They are foreign to you and are not what you are. They are not what you are comfortable with.

Then there are those things which pertain to your culture. You will dream things that line up with your culture. We looked in the first chapter on dreams how Nebuchadnezzar dreamt of the idol, how the king of Egypt dreamt of the cows and the corn. Those things were very prevalent in their day. It was part of their culture.

I do not dream of cows that often, but then again I do not see cows that often, so why would I dream of them? Cows do not mean anything to me. They are not a source of my income. I see them, I tell the kids about them, we drink their milk, but I really do not care much about cows. But in those days, cows were a big part of their lives. They would have dreamt a lot about cows.

We dream about cars; they dreamt about cows. That is the way it is.

You may have dreams where you are driving vehicles and there are certain people driving other vehicles and they are overtaking you. Perhaps you are driving or taking a back seat, but in those days they would probably dream they were on the front of the horse or the back of the horse! It is the way it was. You are going to dream according to your own culture and things that are familiar to you.

There are some societies were they do still use horses and camels and carts. So for them to dream of a horse and a camel and a cart would be perfectly acceptable. But if I had to dream of a horse pulling a cart I would think, "Oh Lord, what's happened to my ministry? I was in a racing car and now I'm in a horse cart! For goodness sake!" But for somebody else who is familiar with that sort of thing, that might speak of a promotion for them. They are thinking, "Hey, I've been upgraded from a donkey to a horse cart!" They might be comfortable with that.

You will have symbols coming up from your spirit that you are familiar with and that are familiar with your culture and your race. It is just like the dream I shared earlier of Craig who dreamt about the rugby. Now, an American would not dream about rugby. In fact, if an American had to dream about rugby he would wake up and go, "Huh? What was that?" He would not dream about rugby because he does not know what rugby is.

He knows football, he knows baseball, he knows soccer, he knows those sorts of sports and he will dream about the things he knows about. The Englishman will dream about cricket, and you will likewise dream about the things you know about. Every culture is different.

You will dreams of scenes in weddings that are familiar to you. In every culture there are different kinds of celebrations. There are different kinds of rituals that we perform. Some things may be familiar to you. But if you had to dream about a wedding or a ceremony that was outside of your culture, it would speak very loudly to you and negatively and say, "Hey, this is out of place. This is out of order. This isn't how we do things."

For that particular culture, however, if they were dreaming of that kind of wedding or that kind of ritual, it would be very commonplace for them. It would be something that is normal and would have a very positive comfortable emotion. It would be a positive connotation, whereas for you it would be negative. However if that person living on the other side of the world had to dream of the way we hold Easter and Christmas, to them it would be negative because it is so alien to them. Can you see how these things all play such an important role?

Here is an example taken from one of our Prophetic School students.

CHAPTER **14**

Examples of Gender and Race

*All nations surrounded me, but in the name of the
Lord I will destroy them.*

~ Psalms 118:10

Chapter 14 – Examples of Gender and Race

Dream:

"In my dream, I was at my house and some other people and I were going to take a trip. I went to get in my car and there was a Muslim girl with a shawl on her head. She got into my car and tried to drive it. I said, "Sorry but only I can drive this car," but she tried to coerce me by being nice to me and saying that I could trust her. In the end I really didn't pay much attention to what she was asking and I just got into my car without even thinking about it and drove off."

Interpretation: By Craig Toach

The car speaks of the ministry that the Lord has given you. The young Muslim woman is clearly not a good picture. Furthermore she is trying to drive your car. She also has a shawl, and although it is a common dress item for young unmarried Muslim to wear, I feel that in the natural it is covering and preventing the true person from being seen. This is much like when you go to a Masked Ball.

It is clear that there is something in your life that is not of the Lord that is trying to drive your ministry. It is preventing its true identity from being seen. The danger is that it is trying to take over you ministry. However, in the dream you did not fall for the ploys and you got into the car and drove off.

I feel that it could be a healing dream with a slight warning to it. I believe it has to do with the masks that you have been battling with. You have overcome them and can see the subtle ploy of the enemy to take over the ministry the Lord has given you. Just be careful of the false religion that could try and influence your ministry.

Doctrinal Stand

Then finally, your doctrinal stand will play a very important role in how you have internal dreams and visions. If you do not believe in the baptism of the Holy Spirit, I very much doubt you will be dreaming about fire and water and such symbols that pertain to that specific stand, unless you are prophetic. However, I am just talking about internal dreams now. You will not dream about things that you do not know about. If you were brought up as a Southern Baptist, had a very strict upbringing and you have never even heard of the baptism, you will not dream about symbols that are synonymous with the baptism of the Holy Spirit, because they are not familiar to you. They are something alien to you. You have never heard about them.

The Lord will use things that you are familiar with to get His message across. If you are really strong in the Word, He will use symbols like bread and wood and gold and the cross, and things that you know about, depending on your doctrinal stand. It will depend on the symbols that are going to be used in your dreams.

Being very prophetic and pretty much open to a lot and any of the moves of God, I receive a whole lot of different kinds of symbols and revelations. There is no limitation to the amount of pictures that the Holy Spirit can give me. Because my mind has been broadened to so many different doctrinal stands and so many different denominations, He can use so many different things.

However, when I dream about a rosary bead it has a negative impression for me. This would represent a religious archetype to me, because I do not believe in Catholicism. So if I had to dream about the Virgin Mary or about a rosary bead or something pertaining to Catholicism, that would have a very negative impression. I would say that means idolatry and would mean that something negative has happened in my life.

However, if you are Catholic and you dream of a rosary bead, it would not have a negative connotation to you. That is who you are. That is what you have been brought up believing, so that is what you are going to dream about. It will not have a negative impression, whereas for me it would have a very negative impression.

You must remember that I am speaking about internal dreams here, not prophetic dreams. I am talking about internal dreams from your spirit and words of knowledge pertaining to past and present things in your life.

Prophetic and External Interpretations

Now that we have dealt with internal symbols let's take a look at the prophetic and external dreams and visions. The rules that I have just explained pertain to the internal dream alone. However when we start talking prophetic, the gift of prophecy, seeing visions, the spirit of wisdom and revelation that we have discussed earlier, a whole new set of rules apply. This is because there is a single standard, not like the internal dream, where the interpretation is dependent on the person in question.

Word of God is the Standard

There comes a single standard for revelation received externally and prophetically, and that standard is the Word of God. This is because it is coming as a supernatural impartation. You see, when the Holy Spirit gives you a supernatural impartation of revelation, He bypasses your templates. He does not speak to you through the things that you grew up with. He speaks directly to you through supernatural revelation. This revelation does not come through your gender, or through your race and culture. It comes direct, and it is very common to have somebody dreaming of something or receiving a vision that they cannot interpret because they do not understand the symbols.

If you dream of something totally alien to you, a symbol that you have never seen or heard of before, it is a prophetic dream, because the Holy Spirit will give you a supernatural impartation of revelation.

No Gender in Spiritual Realm

The first rule is there is no gender in the spiritual realm. You do not get female spirits and you do not get male spirits, because spirits do not have a physical body. Even angels in the heavenly realm are not based on gender. You do not get 'men' and 'women' angels. How do I know this? Jesus made this statement to the Jews when they questioned him on the ownership of a woman who had been married to more than one man, after the resurrection.

> *"But those who are counted worthy to attain that age, and the resurrection from the dead, neither marry nor are given in marriage;*
>
> *Nor can they die anymore, for they are equal to the angels and are sons of God, being sons of the resurrection." ~ Luke 20:35-36*

There can be no marriage and being given in marriage, for there is no gender description in the spiritual realm. Paul further supported this point in Galatians 3:28 where he says:

> *"There is neither Jew nor Greek, there is neither slave nor free, there is neither male nor female; for you are all one in Christ Jesus."*

There is no sex in the spiritual realm, so when you are receiving prophetic revelation there is no differentiation. You can actually see yourself as a man in a bridal gown and that would not have a negative connotation. If it is an external prophetic revelation, dream or vision, to see a man standing in a bridal gown would have a positive connotation, because if you take that and you apply it to Scripture, what is the obvious interpretation? You are wearing a bridal gown. You have become the Bride of Christ.

Now if you had to dream that as just a plain internal dream; if you as a normal guy had to dream that you were walking around in woman's clothing, that would be very negative. However, prophetically speaking, gender does not count. A man can wear a wedding dress prophetically. I have seen it in the Spirit. Do not laugh. I said to one of our students, "Sidney, my man, you look pretty funny in a wedding dress! But the Lord has His favor upon you!"

In the spiritual realm a woman could very easily be dressed up in a man's armor and still very much line up with the Word of God. Looking at scripture we read of the armor of God, which may mean wearing the helmet of salvation and girding your loins with truth and so forth. A woman can wear armor with prophetic and external revelation. A man can wear a wedding dress and it is perfectly acceptable. A man can have a crown put on his head or a woman can have a crown put on her head. There is no gender differentiation when it comes to the spiritual realm.

Do you see now why it is so important to then identify which is internal and which is external and prophetic? It is vital, because the same set of rules does not apply for both.

No Differentiation in Race

There is no race and culture in the spiritual realm. 1 Peter 2:9 says:

> *"But you are a chosen generation, a royal priesthood, a holy nation, His own special people, that you may proclaim the praises of Him who called you out of darkness into His marvelous light;"*

We are a new people. We are a new creation in Christ. We are not a whole people, we are not ten people, we are not five different races of people, we are **A** (singular) people in Christ. We are all one nation. We are all one culture and that culture is based on the Word of God. Our standard in prophetic and external revelation is always the Word of God, because that is how the Holy Spirit speaks. He will never contradict Himself.

So when you are receiving revelation with regards to culture or if you see somebody who is a different culture to you, it will not necessarily have a negative connotation. Look at when Paul saw the Macedonian standing before him and saying, "Please come and minister to us." This was not negative for him. It was positive. It was a prophetic revelation. It was a pretty straightforward revelation that indicated the Lord wanted him to go to Macedonia and preach the gospel. As in 1 Peter 2:9, there is neither Jew nor Greek, because there is no different between race and culture in the spiritual realm. In Christ's eyes we are all the same.

No Doctrinal Differences

There is no difference in opinions of doctrines when it comes to prophetic revelation. I do not care if you are a Baptist, if you are a Methodist, if you are Pentecostal, Charismatic or Seventh-Day Adventist, I do not care what stand you take. If you receive revelation from the Spirit of God prophetically and externally there is one basis and one standard for that revelation, and that basis is the Spirit of Truth and the Word of God.

I have seen this through the nations as we have trained up several of the fivefold ministries through so many different countries. I have come to see that Seventh Day Adventists in America see the same prophetic symbols as the Baptists in South Africa, who see the same prophetic symbols as the Charismatics in Singapore, who see the same symbols as the Methodists in Russia. It does not matter. It is the universal language of the Spirit, which is always based on the Word of God.

There is no one doctrine that you can stick to when it comes to the spiritual realm, because it is all based on the Word of God and not the precepts of man. The symbols are standard and they stay the same. Gold means God's divine nature. The cross stands for salvation. The blood refers to redemption. These are standard symbols that cut across every single doctrinal stand and every single denomination, because they are based on the Word of God. So when it comes to prophetic revelation, realize that it really does not matter what denomination you are in. It really does not matter what doctrinal stand you have made. It always relates to the Word of God.

Desire for Wisdom

As I have been going through these various symbols perhaps you have been saying to yourself, "I really wish that I had that kind of wisdom. I really wish that I could look at my dreams and I could understand what was going on. I wish I had that spirit of wisdom and revelation." It says in James 1:5:

> *"If any of you lacks wisdom, let him ask of God, who gives to all liberally and without reproach, and it will be given to him."*

It is available to you in Christ Jesus and you can have that wisdom if you will ask Him for it. Every member of the Body of Christ should have that wisdom. They should know the Word. They should know what the Holy Spirit is saying. Could you just imagine if everybody in the Body of Christ had an idea of what the Spirit of God was doing in their lives? There would be unity. There would not be any strife. There would not be contention. You would know the next move the Lord was going to make and your brother would be in agreement with you.

Can you see how vital this is? We are talking about knowing the will and the purpose of God in our lives. If every believer knew the will and purpose of God in their lives, we would all be heading in the same direction. We would be as one Body that walked in time, that had the same heartbeat, that moved in the same direction and that knew one another's hearts. Every single one of us needs to be moving into this realm.

I am not talking about fantastic spirituality. I am just talking about knowing the will and the heart of God. And it is available to every believer. Every believer should be walking in it, because only when every believer is walking in it can the Body of Christ truly rise up and be an example to this world. But while we are nitpicking and arguing and trying to decide who is right and who is wrong, the world is dying and they are looking at us because we are a laughing stock - not knowing whether we are coming or going.

If we would just realize that the Word of God is our standard and that the love of Christ should always be our motivation, doctrinal stands and denominations and our race and culture and gender would all fall away, because we would not be seeing with natural eyes. We would be seeing through the eyes of the Spirit.

When you see through the eyes of the Spirit you see a realm and you see a vision that totally cuts across everything you know and feel in the natural. This is because every template that has been built into you from childhood has been based on the sinful responses to life. You have been ill-treated. The moral codes that have been built into you are the wisdom of man, not the wisdom of God. You have been brought up thinking with the wisdom of this world.

If you could for once start seeing the wisdom of God and looking into the spiritual realm and seeing what He is saying; if every believer could be doing that, we could break through the System of this world that is controlling the Body of Christ. We could wake up that Sleeping Giant and stand as that city on the hill and be an example. We could stretch out our hand in power and cause change to happen in the Body of Christ Universal, and in every tribe and nation.

Back to Communing with God

I am not talking about something that is super-fantastic here. I am talking about taking these principles and making them the basic application for your life. I am talking of getting back to basics. I am talking about going back to what God intended right in the Garden of Eden where Adam and Eve spent time every day speaking with the Lord and communing with Him and saying, "Hey Lord, what shall I do here?"

"How was your day, Adam?"

"Oh, not too bad. I named a couple of animals. I trimmed a few hedges, and Eve and I went for a walk at sunset over there. It was a lovely time by the river."

They were communing with the Lord all the time. And that is the order we should be returning to as members of the Body of Christ. The only way you will be able to do this is if you can interpret the language that the Lord is speaking to you all the time.

It may start in dark sayings and it may start in types and symbols such as I have shared here. Perhaps some of it has been confusing to you. But as you start with this, slowly you will start to develop a face to face relationship where you can hear the Lord as clearly as He hears you. That is the ultimate goal in looking at this entire book on dreams and visions. It is not so much to give you answers, but to encourage you into a personal relationship with the Lord Jesus Christ.

Experiencing the Realm of the Spirit

And it shall come to pass in the last days, says God, hat I will pour out of My Spirit on all flesh; your sons and your daughters shall prophesy, our young men shall see visions, your old men shall dream dreams.

~ Acts 2:17

Chapter 15 – Experiencing the Realm of the Spirit

Spiritual Realm Predominant

In this chapter I will be sharing a lot on personal experiences that I have had in the realm of visions. I am hoping, and I pray that as the Holy Spirit enables me, I will give you an idea, a picture and a desire to reach out and claim these same things for yourself. I will be giving you practical illustrations on how the Lord uses visions in every aspect of our spiritual and daily walk. Personally I cannot go a day without seeing visions in some form. You might think that I am super-spiritual, but that is not true at all. I have just learned to tap into that secret language of God and learned to do it at any time, in any place, whenever I need it.

The Lord is speaking to you all the time. If you can learn to tap into that wisdom at any time you need it, He will always have a word for you and there will always be something that He will have to share. Visions should be a way of life for every believer. It should be something that we live in, because does the Scripture not say that the spiritual realm is greater than the natural realm? Should our eyes not be in the spiritual realm so that we can apply that revelation to the natural realm?

But we have it the other way round. We look at the natural realm, we panic and then we run to the Lord in prayer. It should be the other way round. We should have our eyes so keenly tuned to the spiritual realm that we already see up ahead what is going to happen in the natural realm.

We looked at the function of the spirit in 'Visions: Your Secret Conversation with God', on how the spirit has the capacity to see into the future. Now if our eyes were firmly fixed on the spiritual realm, we would see stumbling blocks and promotions way ahead before they happened, and then in the natural realm we could prepare ourselves for that change that is coming. But instead we find ourselves facing surprises, usually negative ones, in our daily walk. Then we suddenly want to scramble to the Word and scramble to the Lord in prayer for some quick fix solution for our problem, where really we should have been working on it way before it even happened.

It is like the old saying goes, "Prevention is better than cure." This applies to this exact illustration I am using here. You need to have your eyes on the spiritual realm so that you are prepared for what is going to happen in the natural realm, because the spiritual is greater than the physical. It is the original way that God created man.

The Face-to-Face Relationship

If you go right back to the Garden of Eden, you will see that the most important time of Adam and Eve's day was the time when they fellowshipped with the Lord in the cool of the day. It was here that He gave them the instructions that they were to live by.

The most devastating thing for Adam and Eve when they were thrown out of the Garden of Eden was not that they could not eat from the trees anymore. The most devastating thing was not that they could not have such a lush place to live in and now they had to work in the hard ground. The most devastating thing for Adam and Eve when they were thrown out of the Garden of Eden was that they were separated from God, because He was the very breath that they breathed, up until the fall.

But through Christ Jesus that right and that blessing has now been returned to us and we can now, through Calvary, enter into God's original pattern. So that which Adam lost has been restored to us through Christ, just as the Word says that though death came through one man, Adam, so also life and glory comes through one man, Jesus Christ. Now, in Jesus, we have the ability to boldly come to the Throne of Grace and receive that direction, through vision, and through other forms of the gifts, to know what is going to happen in our lives and how to apply that wisdom practically to our lives.

3 Categories of Visions in the Word

There are three main categories of visions, which I will cover here briefly.

1st Category: Impressions on the Mind

> *"And it shall come to pass in the last days, says God, hat I will pour out of My Spirit on all flesh; your sons and your daughters shall prophesy, our young men shall see visions;" ~ Acts 2:17*

The first and most common category of visions are those impressions or pictures that are imprinted on your mind. These are the visions that I have been discussing with you up until now and they are the visions that I will be giving you examples of here. They are in fact the standard way that the Lord speaks to us – in those dark sayings and impressions on our minds. They are the most common to every believer.

2nd Category: Trance Visions

> *"I was in the city of Joppa praying; and in a trance I saw a vision, an object descending like a great sheet, let down from heaven by four corners; and it came to me." ~ Acts 11:5*

The second kind of vision is the trance vision. I am sure that you have seen that in Scripture, where you hear of Peter going up into the rooftop, and the Word says that he went into a trance and saw a blanket come down with unclean animals on it. He was then told to, "Arise and eat."

Now, a trance vision is when all your senses are suspended and you are taken into a different realm. It is like your body is there, but your mind is somewhere else. Your senses are all suspended so that in the vision you can actually see, taste and smell what is going on. The more you experience the realm of the Spirit, and the more you open up your heart to the revelations of God, it is not uncommon at all to start experiencing the realm of the Spirit in all of your five senses.

This is not by any means a very common type of vision but the Lord does often use it to get His message across clearly. This is the vision that many will see when they are slain in the Spirit.

3rd Category: Open Vision

> *"Now the boy Samuel ministered to the Lord before Eli. And the word of the Lord was rare in those days; there was no widespread revelation."*
> *~ 1 Samuel 3:1*

The third kind of vision that is mentioned in Scripture is the open vision. Now, the open vision is very simply an image superimposed on your senses. In other words, to you it looks like something is there, but nobody else can see it. Unfortunately, this is a realm that Satan works very strongly in, and you, I am sure, have heard many spooky stories of people seeing ghosts and phantoms and strange things happening. That is an open vision, when an image is superimposed on your senses.

Example from Scripture

A good example in Scripture is of Saul on his way to Damascus. He was thrown off his horse and saw a bright light, and Jesus appeared to him and said, "Saul, Saul, why are you persecuting Me?" It says in the Scriptures that the men with him heard, but they could not see the man who was speaking to Paul. But yet, when Paul recounts the event later to the king, he says, "I saw the Man." He saw Jesus. Jesus appeared to him. It was an open vision and it was to Paul alone. The men with him could not see it.

Another good example of this type of vision is when Jesus was baptized by John the Baptist in the River Jordan.

> *"And the Holy Spirit descended in bodily form like a dove upon Him, and a voice came from heaven which said, You are My beloved Son; in You I am well pleased." ~ Luke 3:22*

You hear of how John says, "The Holy Spirit told me when I see a dove descend on someone, that He is the chosen one, that He is the Son of God." You know the story of how Jesus came to him to be baptized and John saw the dove descend on Jesus. Nobody else saw that dove descend on Jesus, contrary to the popular Bible stories. Nobody saw it, because directly after that John stood up and said, "I have seen the dove, and this has been a sign to me as the Lord said it would be."

Later on Jesus Himself said that John the Baptist was sent as a witness, that He was the Son of God.

Not Common Today

Trance visions and open visions are not as common today. Why is that? It is very simply because in the Old Testament they did not have the indwelling of the Holy Spirit. In those days they did not have the capacity to receive revelation from the Holy Spirit, from their own spirits, because their spirits had been separated by God through the fall of Adam. Jesus had not yet come and breached that gap between man and God, so what had to happen is the prophet in question, had to come to a place of righteousness, before God could then reach down and give him some form of revelation.

Very often the revelation that was given to the prophets was either in dreams, open visions or trance visions. The Lord had to actually suspend their senses to give them His message, because they were not capable of hearing from their own spirits. They were not capable of discerning the spirits for themselves, because they did not have the indwelling of the Holy Spirit.

So for the Lord to make His message very clear He had to literally grab hold of them, suspend all their senses, suspend everything and imprint His message on their minds. You see, the revelation they received was based on their righteousness, because God could not dwell with sinful man. Today, however, thanks to the cross and Calvary, things have changed and we can hear from the Spirit of God any time we need to hear from Him. We do not have to wait until we are standing in a place of external righteousness for the Holy Spirit to bombard us and come upon us suddenly and give us a message. We can just reach out by faith any time we want to and say, "Lord, I'm here. What do you want to say to me today?" And He will speak to you.

The Use of Visions

Visions, like any of the other gifts, are for the sole use of the edification and exhortation of the Body of Christ. This is where dreams and visions differ. Dreams, everybody can have. Even unbelievers dream. But when it comes to visions, they are a supernatural gift from the Holy Spirit that is given to His Body to bring it to maturity through the use of faith, hope and love. How do I know this? 1 Corinthians 12:7 says:

> *"But the manifestation of the Spirit is given to each one for the profit of all."*

The manifestation or the gifts of the Spirit are given to every single member of the Body of Christ so that the entire Body may be edified. That means you. Everyone means you. It means the Lord has given you the ability to have the gifts of the Spirit so that you may be of benefit to the Body of Christ. Visions will be given to you for two reasons – for the edification of yourself, and for the edification of the other members of the Body of Christ.

I can almost hear you saying to me, "But I thought that the gifts were given for the Body. How can visions be used to edify myself?"

Well, are you not part of the Body of Christ? The last time I checked I was part of the Body of Christ, so it means that visions edify me. When Paul speaks of tongues, he says, "We speak in tongues that we might be edified." Does that seem selfish? No. It is not selfish. It is a spiritual gift. That is why it is called 'a gift'. When it is your birthday or when it is a special occasion and somebody gives you a gift or a present, what is usually the purpose of that gift? Is the purpose of that gift to try and compel you to do something? Is the purpose of the gift for you to give it away so that you can go without? Or is the purpose of the gift to have something that you can hold onto, use, enjoy and be filled with thanksgiving that you have something so wonderful?

When I give somebody a gift, I expect that they are going to enjoy using it. That is usually why you buy somebody a gift, so that you can bless them and so that they can be filled with peace, joy and gladness. Do you think our Heavenly Father is any different? So as He gave us these spiritual gifts, He gave them as a blessing out of His heart. He gave them for us to have something to feel good about; something that we could use to edify ourselves and to edify the Body of Christ with. In this we could be a healthy and strong Body. We could be a Body that others are jealous of.

When you look at the promises that the Lord gave the Israelites, He said, "Nations will be jealous of you. When you rise up, kings will be drawn to the brightness of your rising." The world should be jealous of us. They should look at our gifts and the jewels that we wear in the spiritual realm and say, "They've got something we don't have."

When you look at a woman whose husband has given her a huge diamond ring you say, "I wish I had a husband like that, that went and bought me such gorgeous jewelry." I know that being a woman, that is the way I feel. If my husband buys me something special you want other women to look and say, "Wow look at that!" You want them to be envious of you.

Well, the world should be envious of the Body of Christ, because our Bridegroom has given us some beautiful gifts that we should be wearing proudly and that we should be showing off to others and saying, "Do you see what He gave me?" That is why the Lord Jesus gave us those gifts, to bless us.

Personal Experiences in Visions

I will be going through some personal experiences and the various ways the Lord has given us visions to help edify us as a team.

CHAPTER **16**

Visions and Warfare

*Casting down arguments and every high thing
that exalts itself against the knowledge of God,
bringing every thought into captivity to the
obedience of Christ,*

~ 2 Corinthians 10:5

Chapter 16 – Visions and Warfare

One of the realms that I use visions constantly is in the realm of warfare. I cannot possibly imagine going into warfare without knowing what I am doing. What fool would run onto a battleground blindfolded? Not even in the natural are humans that stupid, so why do you think that we should be that stupid in the spiritual realm?

You want to attack the enemy and you rise up and you are going to quote those Scriptures and stand on his neck, and you are going to stand on the Word! That is all fine and well, yes you must put on your armor. You must stand girded and strong. But then you do not put a blindfold on and run into a wall. That is just plain daft! You do not even do that in the natural. Why would you do that in the spiritual?

You need to have the Word in your lips, but you have to see what you are aiming the Word at. I have seen Christians who stand up and attack the devil left, right and center. They are yelling and they are binding and they are standing on his neck. And after an hour they are exhausted and the devil is standing there saying, "Huh?" They missed! They shot all their arrows and they missed. They did not hit him where it really hurt, because they did not know where to aim. They did not know how he came in, in the first place so how could they take away the license he is using?

I have shared extensively in Strategies of War how to remove the enemy's works out of our lives. I teach about how we need to find out first where the entrance point of the enemy is so that we can close it off in our lives. You see Satan does not have a right to attack you any which way he pleases. He has to be given license to do so. Now, when you go into warfare and you want to stand against the enemy in your life, you need to find out where he came in before you can stand against him.

How are you going to do that unless you know how to look into the spiritual realm and unless you know how to receive revelation out of your spirit? You can arm yourself with as many Scriptures as you like, but if you do not hit him in the right place, those Scriptures are going way over his head and they are not being as effective and powerful as they could be.

Now that may sound facetious and that may almost sound heretical to you. But it is the truth, and I have seen it. I have seen people stand on the Word. I have seen them go through many attacks in their lives and they think that just by quoting Scripture after Scripture, not even believing it that this is going to overcome what is happening in their lives. They are wrong, because nine times out of ten there is something in their camp that they need to take out. There is a curse in their lives. There is an object in their house that is bringing a demonic influence, that is an open door to the enemy. They have sin in their lives. They have bitterness in their heart that is opening the door wide for the enemy to come in.

Now you can throw as many Scriptures as you like at the enemy, but if you opened up your heart and are opening up the door wide for him to come in, your efforts are not going to stop him. You can quote until you are blue in the face, but if you are inviting him in he has that inroad. You have to find that open door and you have to close it. Then you hit him with the sword, the Word of God. And I want to tell you, one shot and he is down. You are going to exhaust yourself if you are just shooting your arrows blindly.

Attack in the Ministry

We experience this a lot in the ministry we have. We have come under a lot of demonic attack. There have been specific people and demonic groups and cults who have prayed against us, who would like nothing better than to see us go down. They have been demonically inspired. And there have been times when the team has come under tremendous attack and we go, "Huh? What's going on?"

We do not just accept anything from the enemy. We say, "Where did he get in? The devil's not allowed in this camp unless he's been given license to get in this camp." And the first thing we do is go to prayer and we say, "Okay, Lord, show us the open door."

There have been times where we have unwittingly invited and allowed into our midst, false prophets, and as they have entered the camp they have brought their curse and their demons with them. Strife and conflict erupt amongst the students and negative things start happening in the spiritual realm and we go, "What is going on?" And so as we come to prayer we will see an occult demon and we will know immediately, "Something's up. Somebody's in our midst that is not of the Spirit of God, and they're bringing a curse."

When I see an occult demon in the Spirit, he is big, bald, muscular and fairly human looking. He has pointed ears or perhaps horns, like you would see in the fairy tale books. His skin is either green or dark gray. Now this is only a representation of that spirit, because demons do not really have a body, so what may be an indication of an occult spirit to me may look different in the spiritual realm to you – because they are disembodied spirits, as the Scriptures say.

If we come against that entrance point and stand against that person and that occult spirit with the Word of God, he buckles and he has to leave, and he knows he has to leave, because he has been identified. We close that door in the spiritual realm and we stand against him in the name of Jesus and we apply the blood. But you do not go round sprinkling blood everywhere, when you do not know where to sprinkle it in the first place.

When they had a sacrifice in the Old Testament they had it on the altar. They did not throw it around the room. When you are coming against the enemy, when you are coming in warfare, know where you are aiming your weapon and know what to do with it. Do not throw it away wildly. You will look like a fool.

This is one of the most powerful ways that the Lord has used us, and we also war on behalf of others, but I will go into that next as we discuss the edification of the Body of Christ.

Do you have the enemy reigning in your life and are you battling with poverty and sickness and disease and strife? Are you struggling to get into the spiritual realm? Then start asking the Lord now, "Open my spiritual eyes, Father, that I may see where the enemy has come in."

The Lord may show you bitterness in your heart. He may show you a heart that is black. He may show you a heart that is covered with stone and He says, "There's your problem right there. Sort out your stony heart. Sort out your bitterness, and then tell the enemy to go and he has no license to stay."

There might be a sin in your life that is opening the door to the enemy and the Lord could reveal that. There might be an object that you have brought into your home, an idol that you were not aware of that He could bring to your mind. You need to remove the idol and tell the enemy to go, and he will go.

Confrontation with Princes

As the Lord moves us more and higher up we have come into confrontation with various princes of our area. I remember one time specifically when we were in the spiritual realm I saw the strangest site. I saw what looked like a man-type form and he had what looked like horns. I could not quite understand what he was, but the best way I could describe him was the picture I had seen of the matador as in the old myth. He was half man and half bull. I knew it was a high level demon we were coming against. I shared it with the team, and someone confirmed immediately what I had seen and said, "That's the Prince of America."

It just so happened that we had just launched our Schools into the States and we were starting to draw in students and raise them up, and it was causing a bit of a stir. It was causing a ruckus in the spiritual realm. He did not like it too much. His kingdom was getting a little shaken there.

So instead of dealing with the insignificant demons that were annoying us, we went straight to the top and we stood against him in the name of Jesus and told him to lose his hold on the students that the Lord had brought us. He had to go and he had to lose his hold. But we would never have known where the attack was coming from unless we had first seen it in the spiritual realm.

Praise and Worship

The most wonderful experiences I have ever had in the spiritual realm have to be in praise and worship. When I sat down to prepare this chapter and I started letting the revelations flow that the Lord had given me, most of them that came to me were the ones that I had received in praise and worship. There is something about singing and praise and worship that lifts you up into a realm that is not natural.

You know what it is like in a church meeting when the band is playing and that gentle breeze comes in the door and you can feel it tangibly. It is like this warmth, like somebody is pouring oil over you. And when you close your eyes you are lifted up. You are lifted up into a realm that is beyond any human understanding. That is the realm of the Spirit.

And as you praise the Lord and you lift up your hearts, you unite yourself with the heavenly realm, and you unite yourself with the Holy Spirit, and you start being lifted up. As you start being lifted up, that is the time you will most likely receive visions of the heavenly realm.

Angels with Us

It is very common during our praise and worship for us to see the angels singing and dancing with us. We have the most glorious times. The worship angels have wings and are dressed in plain robes like you would expect them to be. They are always aglow with the presence of the Lord, with light hair. I have seen them with tambourines, timbrels, harps, and even some with drums and various stringed instruments. They dance and praise and sing and it is something to see them in the Spirit glorifying the Lord. It motivates you. It lifts you up and makes your heart want to burst.

I want to dance like they do. I want to praise the Lord Jesus with abandon like they do, because they praise with everything they have. They throw their arms in the

air, they spin around, they dance and sing and they clap.
They are so full of the joy of the Lord.

Jesus' Heartbeat

When I see them and I hear them sing in the spiritual
realm, I want to join in with them. I want to dance and
sing and jump up and down. It is such a beautiful
experience and you can have it too, because the spiritual
realm, when you go into praise and worship, is there for
every person. It is there for everyone and it is there to
lift you up and let you know that there is something
beyond the natural. It gives you hope. It lets you see that
there is indeed joy and peace in this life we call the
Christian walk.

The minute you take your eyes off the natural realm,
that is when your problems go away. When we have
gone through the most difficult times we have gone to
the Lord and said, "Lord, what's going on?" Then we
enter into praise and worship. I will often see the Lord
Jesus in vision. He loves to dance and He has a good
sense of humor. He will come up to me and take me by
the hand and say, "Come, let's dance."

"Oh but Lord, I really feel depressed. You won't believe
the day I've had. The kids have been driving me nuts, I
have been picked on. I've been getting emails pouring in
my ears. The students have been giving me a hard time. I
want to just curl up and die."

He says, "Ah, forget it! Come and dance." He will take
me by the hand and we will turn around and we will

dance, and by the end of it I have forgotten the worries of that day. They are so far away, because He has lifted up my spirit. He says, "Hey, you're something special to Me."

So when I enter into praise and worship that has to be the revelation and the vision that I see the most, of my Heavenly Bridegroom, Jesus, coming and taking my hand and dancing with me. He has given me such lovely illustrations during these intimate times. He said to me once, "You know, speaking to others and walking in your daily walk and learning to flow from your spirit is like a dance with Me. If I hold you really close and you put your head on My chest, you can hear My heartbeat." He said, "All you need to do is step in time with My heartbeat." But to step in time with His heartbeat I have to keep my head on His chest.

That is really what the experience of the spiritual realm is. It is having your ear to the heartbeat of God, to know when He wants to move how He wants to move and where He wants to move. That is the place that every believer should be coming to, just like I shared in the opening passage.

There will come a time when you will know Him like He knows you. Just like you are known, you will know. Is that not really the ultimate goal of receiving revelation and experiencing the realm of the Spirit? Is the ultimate goal not to hear the heartbeat of God?

Developing Your Relationship with God

17 Now the Lord is the Spirit; and where the Spirit of the Lord is, there is liberty.

18 But we all, with unveiled face, beholding as in a mirror the glory of the Lord, are being transformed into the same image from glory to glory, just as by the Spirit of the Lord.

~ 2 Corinthians 3:17-18

Chapter 17 – Developing Your Relationship with God

This takes me to my next most favorite topic, and that is that visions develop your relationship with the Lord. Do you remember when you were dating how you and your boyfriend used to sit and talk the biggest load of rubbish for hours and you never got bored? Being a woman, I could sit on the phone for hours and never get bored. Craig however, he did not like the phone so much, so after twenty minutes that was his limit. But I could go hours and just talk and talk and talk. I bet you did not notice, hey? I can go on for ages just talking.

When you first meet it is like you can just never find enough to talk about. You talk about the weather, you talk about your desires, and you talk about your dreams, your aspirations, your past and your future. When you are dating it seems like the whole world is out there for you to conquer. You have so many ideas, so many plans of what you are going to do with your life and what path your life is going to follow.

Visions are like having that conversation with the Lord Jesus. And if you would just give Him the time, He would talk your ear off. He would give you so many pictures and aspirations and desires and goals that He has for your life that you would not be able to shut Him up. He has so much for you. He wants you to know Him as a friend, so that you can get to know Him as a lover, so that you can get to know Him as your Bridegroom.

Personal Vision of the Lord Jesus

Visions are really just the starting point to entering into that relationship. I will never forget the first time I met the Lord Jesus face to face. We were in praise and worship (you can see now why praise and worship is so special to me), and at the time I had felt really convicted. I felt, "Lord, I'm just me. I'm so insignificant. I look at everything You've done and You're so great. You're so awesome."

As we had entered into praise and worship we had entered into the Throne Room and I had bowed down. In the spiritual realm I opened my eyes and I saw in front of me a pair of feet and they had holes in them. I knew immediately who this was. This was Jesus. I was in the Throne Room and He was sitting on His Throne and I was on my face in front of His feet.

He bent down and I almost felt like, "You know, you're not really supposed to look at the Lord. He is so holy, He is so magnificent, He is so awesome and you are supposed to fear Him and revere Him," and I was almost afraid to look up. But He took His hand and He put it under my chin and tilted my head up so that I could look Him directly in His eyes.

I do not think I will ever forget the expression on His face. He looked right through me and He knew everything about me. Yet He was still proud of me and

He still loved me. He knew everything about me, but He still loved everything about me. He was average in height and build with medium brown, shoulder length hair. He didn't have a beard and His features were distinct and sharp. When looking at Him I could understand how He would need to have been identified by Judas, because He looked so average in His appearance. I also understood why His disciples could not recognize Him on the road, because He had lost His beard when the soldiers plucked it out.

He picked me up and He made me stand on my feet and He took me by the hand and said, "Come." I walked with Him and I was not quite sure where we were going at first, but as we walked I could hear the sound of water. I looked around me and He had taken me to this beautiful green meadow. In this meadow was a river, a gentle stream. It was gentle enough to give off that sound of water trickling over the rocks.

Next to the river was a huge willow tree. Willow trees have a lovely template for me. When I was a child we had a huge willow tree in our front yard and I used to spend hours there by myself, just lying under this tree, smelling the grass and daydreaming. Little did I know, that right back there the Lord was speaking to me in my heart. When I look back now, I know that He was speaking to me. So as He took me underneath the branches of that tree, the familiar feeling of childhood and security and being in a place where I was in my own world all came flooding back.

This time however, He sat with me. He said to me, "This is our secret place." It was as if I was a little child and I crawled up onto His lap and He just held me. He did not need to say anything to me and I did not need to say anything to Him, because He just knew. He knew what I felt. He knew what I needed, and right at that time I just needed Him to hold me. As I cuddled up on His lap I could smell His clothes and they smelt like the earth after it has rained. It is the same as when you wake up early in the morning at the crack of dawn and there is that smell in the air. He smelt like all the good things of my childhood.

I cannot possibly explain to you how it felt, but it changed my life. For the first time I met Jesus. I met Jesus, the man. I met Jesus, my best friend. And every time after that, after I came to prayer, He was there waiting for me, and I only needed to close my eyes and He was there. He was always there in our secret place. And if I was having a hard time and if I was really stressed out, all I needed to do was to go to a quiet place and close my eyes and say, "Jesus," and He was there, waiting in our secret place.

The grass was always green and the water was always clear. And even today, when I think back on that memory, it stirs something inside of me. It stirs that familiar feeling of being loved and accepted and feeling safe. So if there is nothing else I can impress on you through this chapter, it is that the Lord wants to draw you into the secret place. It may look different to mine, but it does not matter. He has a secret place just for you and Him, where He wants to talk to you. You can have it, and you can have it right now.

Direction

Another area where the Lord uses visions in our spiritual walk is to give us spiritual direction. We do not take a step in this ministry without first receiving direction from the Lord. We come together as a group, we go apart as individuals, and then we share our individual revelations, then the Lord will give us revelation again as a group. So we will know which step to take next.

Personal Direction

Very often we will see various paths and roads in the Spirit. Often the Lord has shown us what lies up ahead on our spiritual journey. On one occasion I saw a vision of us walking along a path and ahead I saw a detour that went off to one side. The Lord was saying, "You're on a path now, but you're about to hit a dusty road and you are going to go onto a detour. Do not worry about it, though, for it is of Me."

This happened when we had to suddenly move homes and we did not know what was going on. We had to move into a smaller home because we could not find anything else and everything looked like it was falling apart. Things were not coming together, we were frustrated and we said, "Lord, what's going on?"

He said, "Don't worry about it. You're on a detour. But at the end of the detour I am going to bring you onto a wider road. This is part of your training."

So we stuck it through, and it was about a three month span and it was a very hard time for us. It seemed like all hell was let loose against us. Things were very difficult. But you see, we had that vision in our hearts and we knew, "Hang on, we're still in the Lord's will. We didn't miss it somewhere."

Then came the time for us to move again and we moved into a much bigger home and the ministry took off like we had never seen it take off before. It was there that we saw the road widen right ahead of us. But if we had not seen that detour ahead of time we would have lost hope. We would have thought that we had gone off the path, but the Lord had already forewarned us. We knew what was happening and could say, "Okay, let's press on and follow through. The wider path is very soon."

Direction for Ministry

The Lord also gives us direction with regards to our ministry. There was a time where I was flowing very strongly in the prophetic ministry and the Lord said, "Okay, time to change emphasis. Here's a sword."

I said, "I don't know Lord, I'm kind of getting used to this key, this prophetic key."

He said, "Throw away the key. Here's the sword. Use My Word. Become a teacher!"

Suddenly everything that was in me from the prophetic side died and I knew why it had died, because the Lord was saying, "Leave the prophetic now, I want to train you in the teaching side. You can get back to that later." But had I not seen that ahead of time in the spiritual realm, when my prophetic gifts started to wane and the Lord did not manifest them through me so much I would have panicked and thought I was missing it. But when the prophetic started to wane I knew exactly what was happening. The Lord was twisting my arm and saying, "Okay, move a bit faster now! Let it go."

That was a bit of a tough one to go through, but He was very convincing as only He can be. However had I not seen it in the spiritual realm, I would not have known what was happening in the natural realm.

Vision of Ministry Call

I would like to share with you the vision the Lord gave me concerning my future in ministry. Even in the toughest times it has helped keep my eyes directly on the goal ahead. The Lord showed me that I was on a path that was in the middle of nowhere. I had a backpack on, it was not territory that I had ever seen before or a place that I had ever been before. I was hiking through mountains, hills and valleys. It is as though I was going where nobody had ever been before and I was making a path as I was going. I was stumbling over stones and getting stuck with thorns. I should have known it symbolized my prophetic preparation!

I was going through this trail and it was really hard work, but the Lord kept saying, "Press on through, press on through." Well, I pressed on through and went over hills and mountains and valleys and rivers, and then all of a sudden it looked as though I had come a full circle and was now standing back at the starting point.

I said, "Lord, and now what?"

As I looked to my left I saw a whole group of people and He said to me very clearly, "You have learned how to conquer this trail. You have learned what path is the best to follow. Now take the trail you have built and take the knowledge you have gained and teach it to others!"

As He said that I remembered how at one stage there was a great big canyon ahead of me. I had to build a bridge by myself to get across it to the other side. Then He said, "Now this is what you are going to do," and I saw myself back with this group of people. As I walked again the path that I had gone before, I saw some of those people follow behind me and they followed in the path that I had made. But then I saw that there were some that were reluctant to follow and were still sitting on the shoreline, so I carried those reluctant little ones over the bridge with me.

Then there was a third of the group still remaining, and those I took and showed them how to make the bridge. I taught them how to blaze the trail that I had just made. The Lord, through that vision, showed me very clearly three aspects of my ministry. He said, "You're going to stand as an example and others will follow you. But there will be those who will be wounded and hurt." He said, "Those, you will have to pick up and carry. But there will a small group of those whom I will send you that you will teach to do what you are doing, and then they themselves will go out and blaze their own trails."

That gave me hope for my entire ministry and it will be with me until the day I die, because that is my purpose in life. That is my mandate and my goal and vision. And it is like I shared in the chapter on visions, without a vision the people perish. Without a vision, you have no hope for the future.

Edification of the Body

And if one member suffers, all the members suffer with it; or if one member is honored, all the members rejoice with it.

~ 1 Corinthians 12:26

Chapter 18 – Edification of the Body

Visions are largely used for the edification of the Body, just like we said earlier. I have heard so many prophets say, "You know I just don't understand it. I have so many dreams and visions, but I can't seem to interpret them. But yet, let anybody else give me their dream or vision and I can interpret it so easily."

That is very simple to explain. Gifts are given for us to pour out. The first purpose of all the gifts is for us to pour out to others first. It is for the use of others. And yes, they are for our edification like I have shared, but it begins with us pouring out to others, because that is really what the Lord gave us the gifts for, that we might edify one another. You see when we edify one another we build unity, and that is the Lord's ultimate goal, for us to stand as a single Body.

So the ideal thing for you to do is to take this book and share it with a friend, and then for the two of you to share one another's dreams and visions, and then interpret for one another. You will find it way easier to interpret the dreams and visions of your friend, particularly if they are prophetic, than you will for yourself. Why is that?

I have come to find that their faith literally draws the interpretation out of you. The gifts are operated by faith, and when somebody comes to you in faith and says,

"Please help me interpret this vision," they literally suck the interpretation out of you. I can feel this when I go into a chat or when I am with a group of people that really desire ministry and they look to me and are expecting me to minister to their needs. They know that if they say to me, "Please pray with me about this," that their need will be met.

Now I am not so great and wonderful that I meet their needs. No, they come to me and the Holy Spirit meets their needs through me, because He is faithful and He is moved by faith. He will simply use me as that vessel to meet their need, because their faith required that their need be met. That is why the Lord allows us to meet one another's needs in the Body of Christ, that we may pour out to each other.

Illustration of the Vine

It is just like the vine that Jesus described at the Last Supper in John. He said, "I am the vine and you are the branches." At the end of the branches are fruit. What we are supposed to do is take what the Lord gives us and draw it from Him and put it through our branches so that we can produce fruit.

Well, your brother branch is sitting at the end of your branch. Pour into him and he will pour into the next guy, and he will pour into the next guy. Then when people come and look at this vine called the Body of Christ they will see the fruit on it. They will see it, because we have poured into one another. We took the life from the root, which is Christ, and we poured that life into one another. And because we poured that life into one another, that life is going to bear fruit. When the world looks at us they will see that fruit.

But I tell you what, you come to a vine that has got green ugly grapes on it, or no grapes at all, you do not think much of that vine. But yet, when you see a vine with big juicy grapes on it, you think, "Wow, what wonderful fruit." Notice you do not say, "Wow, what wonderful branches." No, you say, "Wow, what wonderful fruit!"

What we should be aiming for in the Body of Christ is to produce fruit in one another. And if you would pour into your brothers and sisters by receiving from the Lord first, the Body of Christ will bear fruit, and we are going to stand as an example to this world.

Intercession

The most powerful way that the Body is edified is through intercession, with us standing in the gap for one another. Intercession is primarily the domain of the prophet, but everybody can move in the ministry of intercession. However, if you have been used extensively in intercession, it is indeed the hallmark of the prophet, and it indicates a higher calling on your life.

Releasing for Others

There are many times I have stood in the gap for others, where I see open doors in their lives where the enemy is getting in, and I will be led to close those doors. Or I will see them in chains and I will be led to break them.

Or perhaps a person has specifically been releasing their faith for finance and they are on their knees saying, "Lord, please we need finance." There have been times when I have seen a door of provision in the Spirit and the Lord will say, "Open that door for him." And so, in the spiritual realm I will release that provision for them in prayer and intercession.

Somebody could perhaps be praying to the Lord concerning an illness, and their faith will release the Holy Spirit to move on me and say, "Release it. Release that health for them," and I will stand up and use the authority of the prophet that the Lord has given me, and I will unlock that door to their healing. They will be touched and healed.

Angels and Demons

It is very common to see angels and demons in intercession – angels more often, because you are often led to release angels on behalf of others. Sometimes this is for protection, sometimes for help, blessing or assistance. There are many times that we have seen angels in the Spirit, other than the worship angels, which I shared about last time. We often see warrior angels, which are sent to do war on behalf of others.

Warrior angels are very strong looking characters. They very often wear colorful sashes or types of armor, they always carry a sword and they have red fiery eyes. They are very foreboding looking people. I would not like to cross their paths. But I know that when I see such an angel in the Spirit the Lord is saying, "Release the decree so that My angels may war on behalf of your brother and sister."

Perhaps I will have a messenger angel come. Messenger angels are very ordinary looking. They are about the size of an average man, they dress like your typical stereotyped angel, in a white robe with light shining round them, and they usually come with a scroll. I know when I see such an angel that the Lord is saying, "I have a word that I want you to speak." It is usually a word of exhortation.

Sometimes I will see a messenger angel as well, but he will have a trumpet, and I will know, "Hey, the Lord wants me to speak a decree. He wants me to speak into being something He has designed for a specific person and for His Body in particular."

So angels and demons are something you will very often experience in intercession if the Lord has been leading you into that arena.

Counseling

I could not give a single word of counsel without experiencing the realm of the Spirit, because not every person is the same. You cannot carve people's problems in stone, because the Lord has made us as individual members of the Body of Christ. What is a solution for one person is not a solution for another, and that is the mistake that many people make. They think, "Well, if I had this problem in my marriage and it was solved this way, therefore if another person has a problem that looks similar, they must solve it the way I did, naturally!"

Wrong! Every person has a different need and a different root to their problem. I could not possibly counsel without the Spirit of the Lord. This I use very often when I am evaluating a student with regards to their ministry. The Lord will tell me the roots and the problems and issues in their lives that they need to deal with before they can move on in ministry, and what has been holding them back.

Very often I will see a heart with walls around it and I will know, "This person has built walls around themselves so that nobody will hurt them, but unfortunately it has also stopped the Lord from being able to reach in and progress them in their ministry."

Ministry of Inner Healing

This is the most powerful way in which visions are used. In the ministry of inner healing there have been times where there have been people who have been so rejected and hurt in life and they have built so many of those walls around their hearts. They have literally imprisoned themselves to the extent where they cannot even show love to their husband, their wife or their children.

They have built so many walls to try and protect themselves from hurt and pain, because of the hardships of life that they cannot even show affection to those closest to them. There is a cry within, and inside they really desperately love and they desperately want to show it, but they cannot. There is something blocking it. Unfortunately that blockage also stops them from loving the Lord and from the Lord reaching in and touching them.

In such times Craig and I have both ministered very effectively to such people by taking them back to the original time of that hurt. We will usually see the child at the age the first hurt occurred, the first rejection or the first pain. So by revelation of the Spirit the Lord will show us the child at the age of four or five or whatever age the child was when the hurt first began. The Lord will then lead us to take that little child and lead them out of that prison and into the sunlight. And as they step into the sunlight they are instantly released from those chains. The Holy Spirit then supernaturally reaches in and brings healing and change to that inner child who has been crying out and hurting, and even now as an adult they are still hurting as that child.

The Holy Spirit reaches in and He picks them up and says, "Okay, that first hurt, that first link in the chain that has caused all your pain – I'm shattering it." And as they face that rejection, as they face that first fear, that first bad situation, as they are forced to look at it, the Holy Spirit comes in and He brings a miraculous healing.

Now we could not do that if we did not have the revelation in the spiritual realm. We would not know where to start. We would be digging around in their adolescent years; we would be digging around from conception. We would never have known unless the Spirit of God had revealed to us, "This is your starting point. This is the root. Deal with it!"

Deliverance

The Lord uses visions in the ministry of deliverance. This is also a very powerful way in which the Lord gives us revelation into setting His people free from demonic bondage. I have often seen where people have had curses very prevalent in their lives, particularly if they have been generational curses. I will see a person standing with cords attached to them and their father. If the generations go back further, I may actually see sets of men or women, depending on which side it relates to. By seeing this kind of vision, I will be able to say, "This generational curse stems back so many generations."

Sometimes the cord goes so far back into the past that I cannot possibly see it and tell them how many generations it goes back, but usually I will be able to see how far it goes back. Usually I will say, "This problem, this curse, this occult activity that you are experiencing comes from your grandfather."

They will usually say something like, "You know what? My grandfather was a medium. He was involved in witchcraft or divination."

I can know that, without them having to tell me a thing about themselves. And usually this helps with people who do not want to tell you their secrets and they have so many skeletons in the closet and do not know where to start. You can say, "This is the root of your problem. This comes from your great-grandmother," and they say, "You know, I've been told stories about her. She was involved in a false religion."

Then we know, "Yes, that's the source of the problem." We break those generational links, we send back those curses in Jesus' name and the person is set free instantly, because we have dealt with the root.

There have been times when people have been involved in occult activity in their youth, perhaps even something minor that they have forgotten about, in which case we will see it in the Spirit and say, "Hang on a minute. I see you around 'this' age and something happened around that time. Does anything stand out to you concerning that time of your life?"

They say, "You know what? At that age I met this friend and we started going to a couple of séances, but I didn't think it was a big deal."

We go, "Bingo! That's the problem."

We deal with it, they close the door, break the links and they are delivered. We could not possibly carry out deliverance without that kind of knowledge.

Physical Healing

The Lord uses us very visually in physical healing. We would lay hands on anybody and tell them what exactly is wrong with them physically.

This happened once with the landlord of one of the homes we lived in. He had a heart condition and none of the doctors could find out what the matter was with him, but his health was becoming worse and worse. As my dad prayed for him he said, "There's something wrong with one of your arteries," and he explained to him exactly how the artery looked, where the blockage was, and what was happening.

Not too long after that the landlord came back to us and said, "You know what? You were right. The doctors finally found the source of the problem and it was exactly like you said it was."

How powerful! The Holy Spirit can reach in right there. I have found that this kind of revelation has been more powerful even than actual healing, because a lot of the time when you feel sick in your body, it is the fear of what is wrong with you that is more damaging than the sickness itself. So for us to lay hands on somebody and say, "Oh, don't worry about it. It's just a cold or a mild infection and it will clear up," is usually more powerful than an actual healing a lot of the time.

Also, when you know the source of the problem, you can speak directly to it. When somebody comes to you with a hundred symptoms, you could not possibly say what is wrong with them. They say, "I don't know what's wrong with me. I'm just sick."

We can lay hands on them and say, "You have a kidney infection. We speak to those kidneys now. In the name of Jesus you will come right, right now!" That is the power of visions, and this is something that you can move in as well.

Most Important – Agape Love

I would like to conclude with a famous passage. I will begin from 1 Corinthians 12:31. It says:

> *"But earnestly desire the best gifts. And yet I show you a more excellent way."*

1 Corinthians 13:1-2

> *"Though I speak with the tongues of men and of angels, but have not love, I have become sounding brass or a clanging cymbal.*
>
> *And though I have the gift of prophecy, and understand all mysteries and all knowledge, and though I have all faith, so that I could remove mountains, but have not love, I am nothing."*

The gifts of the Spirit are really the door to the spiritual realm. And when you walk through that door, you will find the agape love of Jesus Christ on the other side. That is our ultimate goal, to walk, talk and be with Jesus. To be in tune with Him; to move as He moves and have our heads on His chest, that we may hear and feel His heartbeat.

Your ultimate goal in earnestly desiring spiritual gifts is so that you may know and may live in and you may pour out that agape love, which is indeed more supernatural than any vision, than any experience that you can have in the spiritual realm. To know His agape love and to know it as you are known is more powerful than any experience in the Spirit. And if you would earnestly desire it, it is there for you right now.

I want you to reach out and claim it now in Jesus' name. If you would earnestly desire it the Holy Spirit will move upon you right now to give you those things that your heart desires, because He desires that you receive the gifts. He desires that you have the gift of the spirit of wisdom and revelation. He desires that you have the gift of agape love so that you might be a shining example to the world.

"Holy Spirit I pray right now that You would move upon Your people, and as the desires of their hearts have been stirred up through this chapter that You would indeed raise them up and give them a spirit of revelation, so that they might know you, as you know them. That they may see with eyes, not through a dark glass anymore, Father, but see clearly into the spiritual realm, that they would know what the future holds for them; that they would know what the present holds for them.

And most importantly, Lord Jesus, that they would know You as You know them. That they may hear Your heartbeat, that they may dance with You in that intimate embrace. That they may walk through this life victorious and bold and confident in what You have placed in them. That they might indeed know what it means to be a son or daughter of the Most High God. That they may stand in that knowledge, authority and wisdom. That they may be a city that is set on a hill as an example to the nations. I pray for it, in Jesus' name. Amen."

Interpreting for Others

7 If you abide in Me, and My words abide in you, you will ask what you desire, and it shall be done for you.

8 By this My Father is glorified, that you bear much fruit; so you will be My disciples.

~ John 15:7-8

Chapter 19 – Interpreting for Others

Bearing Fruit

We have been looking at how you can interpret your own dreams and visions, but wouldn't you like to be able to interpret the dreams and visions of others? Wouldn't you love it if your friends and your family could come to you for the answers to their dreams and visions? Where you are at the place in your walk with the Lord where you knew His heartbeat to the extent where you are not just receiving revelation for yourself any longer, but you are now beginning to pour out and give that same revelation on behalf of others. Is that not after all the desire that the Lord put in each and every one of us – to minister to each other?

John 15:7-8 says:

> *"If you abide in Me, and My words abide in you, you will ask what you desire, and it shall be done for you.*
>
> *By this My Father is glorified, that you bear much fruit; so you will be My disciples."*

Is that not after all the end goal in being a believer? It is to bear much fruit. And in bearing much fruit, is it not the end goal to bear that fruit in others? Is the Body of Christ not set up after all, that we would pour into one another, that as that vine, we could be fruit for the Lord Jesus? He is the vine and we are the branches.

As you have come to receive the interpretation and revelation for yourself, wouldn't it be so exciting to see that revelation being poured out to others? To not just see the direction and fruit in your life, but to also see the fruit in the lives of your brothers, your sisters, your family, your friends, and know that you somehow had a part to play in the fruit that is being revealed in their lives.

Personally there is no greater reward for doing the work of the Lord than seeing your fruit being borne in somebody else. And that is what this entire chapter is about – about bearing your fruit in others. It is not for you just to be a hotshot and to have all the answers, but to take the revelation and the interpretation and to see it working in the life of somebody else. To see the revelation changing their lives and meaning something to them; to see it encouraging them and giving them faith, hope and love. To see them take that revelation and run with it.

Six Pointers for Ministering

Doesn't it burn in you? It burns in me, and I am going to show you just how you can take that revelation and put it in others. But before I give you any practical examples I want to take you through a couple of pointers that you need to keep in mind when ministering to another. These pointers are not restricted simply to dream interpretation, but to ministry in general, because you must realize that you may just begin ministering to others in interpretation. However it does not stop there. As you make yourself trustworthy in the small things, the Lord will then expand your horizons and He will begin to use you more and more in ministry.

As you start moving into wider circles of ministry, these principles will remain the same and you will begin to apply them, not just to interpretation, but in prayer and intercession, in psalmody and music, in preaching and in teaching. So let what I am about to share become a foundation in your heart. Let it become a foundation in your life which you are going to base your attitude for ministry on.

1st Pointer: Gifts Work through Faith

The first point you need to remember in any ministry is that all the gifts operate by faith. It is so like human nature to stand back and look at the great men and women of God who are moving in powerful gifts and anointing and to think, "Wow, they must have such tremendous faith. They must be such incredible specimens of the human race that the Lord can do such miracles through them."

This is partly true. Partly they do have that much faith, but mostly it is the faith of those who come to receive that activate the gifts in them. It is not their great faith that causes the gifts to function in their ministry. It is the great faith of the people who look up to them and take that gift from them, and desire that gift to be operated in them that makes that gift work.

Example of Jesus

Do you think I am speaking heresy? Let's take a look at Jesus. You do not get a greater man of faith than that. He was perfect, but yet He said the strangest thing when He went to His hometown. He said, *"A prophet is not accepted in his hometown."* Then the Scripture goes on to say that He did no miracles there, except He just healed a few sick people.

The Lord was astounded at their lack of faith. And even the Son of Man, Jesus Christ Himself, could not do miracles in His hometown. Why? Because the people did not have faith in Him! Was there something wrong with Jesus' faith? No, He was perfect. But not even He could impose the healing and the miracles into their lives. The gift would not operate through Him without their faith.

I will never confess that it is my great gifts and my great abilities that allow me to get revelation and interpretations. It is for those who look up to me and come to me seeking the answers that the Lord will use this simple vessel to give them the answers that they desire. Because at the end of the day the Lord is faithful, and He will simply use the vessel that has been yielded to Him. It is not the vessel that is of such great honor. It is the spirit within that vessel. And if you stand as a yielded vessel, as people come to you and look up to you for answers, the Lord will use you. It is His power that will be manifest and it will be their faith that has motivated that power. It will not be your faith and it will not be your great ability. So set your mind very straight on that right now, that unless others look up to you and receive from you, the gifts will not work because they operate by faith.

2nd Pointer: Living Each Lesson

The next point that you are bound to experience very early in training for ministry is that you live each lesson. For anybody who has been on the road of ministry for just a little while, you will learn that you live every lesson you teach. You cannot teach or share and you cannot be an exhorter concerning things you know nothing about. So before you can stand up and actually preach something, you need to learn it first.

Our ministry team has learned this one in a very practical way. And even now, as I came to prepare this book on dreams, we started living each chapter as I was presenting them. Deception and nightmares was not a nice chapter to relive! We all started having nightmares! For me to reteach afresh from the Spirit of God, I had to relive the lessons so that when I shared, it would be relevant. It was fresh bread out of the oven. It was not stale bread that had been sitting on the shelf and had gotten all moldy over the years. It was something that was new and living water within, so that as I came to minister, it would pour out in freshness and power.

As you come to interpreting for others, you are going to live each lesson yourself. You will live the praise, you will live the petition, and you will live the intercession. You will live the deception and the nightmares. Because until you can understand and have lived it in your own life, you will not be able to then pour it out and live it in the lives of others.

So, if by this point in the book, you have already begun experiencing some of the chapters, do not be concerned, because it is very normal. In fact, after publishing just a few of the chapters for others to read, I had many feedbacks from people saying they suddenly started having dreams and visions again that they had not had in years. Suddenly the gifts that had been dormant in them were starting to stir up and they were living it as I was ministering it to them. As they were living it, they in turn were able to minister it to others.

So if you are excited about being able to minister this to somebody else, then be prepared to stand in those shoes of experience first, because before you are going to minister it to them, you will live it yourself!

3rd Pointer: Keep Your Stream Clear

The third point to remember is to keep your stream clear. It is very important that you keep that internal stream of yours clean on a continual basis. This is vital because the more it becomes bogged down with junk and curses such as fear, bitterness, anger and the daily stresses and struggles of life, the more the revelation that you try and speak with will be colored by those pressures, stresses and bitterness' of life.

It is vital to keep that stream clear. Sometimes you get so busy with life and with the ministry and daily activities that you forget to clear the junk from yesterday. You forget to spend time in the presence of the Lord. You forget to speak in tongues and to get into the Word. What happens then is that stream, which was so pure in you before, starts getting bits of debris put in it. It starts getting a couple of leaves and some stones and sand in it. Then suddenly when you want to rise up and minister to somebody else you find that there is an edge off your anointing. Yes, the revelation still comes, but there is something lacking. Before you know it, you are even battling to get revelation for yourself.

4th Pointer: Spirit, Not Mind

The fourth point to keep in mind is that when ministering, use your spirit and not your mind. Revelation comes from the Spirit, not the mind. There is such a temptation to get caught up in intellectual thinking. There is such a temptation to dissect and analyze and to look at everything from every corner, that you actually stop getting revelation from your spirit. What starts coming out is just a load of knowledge and garbage from your mind. Then what you start doing is you begin putting people into packages. And because you have everything neatly laid out in your mind, you start generalizing and you start saying, "Well, this symbol means the same for everyone. And this kind of person will always have this kind of problem. This kind of dream will always have this kind of interpretation."

When you start doing that you are well on your way to deception. The Word of God says that, ...*the natural man does not receive the things of the Spirit of God, for they are foolishness to him; nor can he know them, because they are spiritually discerned. (1 Corinthians 2:14)*

You cannot discern revelation from the Spirit with your mind. You discern the revelation of the Spirit of God with your own spirit. Has this not been the entire theme of this book, which is Dream Interpretation by the Spirit, to receive revelation from our spirits? It is to commune with the heavenly realm, to know what the Lord is saying to us on a continual, fresh basis. Every word that comes out of your mouth for every individual must be fresh. It must be new, real and relevant to them for that specific need, for that specific situation.

If you are thinking too much with your mind and trying to figure out the interpretation too much in your head, then you are going to lose it. This is because the mind cannot comprehend the things of the Spirit, and you could overlook a glaring need that the Lord has wanted to minister to in that person. You could actually miss a ministry opportunity. That person could be coming to you with a deep desire and need and has been crying out to the Lord, and by you trying to comprehend everything with your mind, you could miss what the Spirit of the Lord is trying to say to that person. You could miss an amazing and incredible time of ministry that could leave that person's needs met.

Do not go to fill a person's head with knowledge. Go to speak wisdom. The Lord really laid this on my heart as I came to write this book. He said, "You know, more important than knowledge is wisdom. When Solomon came to me when he was still a child he asked me for wisdom." He said, "At that time in his life he did not have any knowledge. He wasn't old enough to know anything yet. But he asked me for wisdom. And when he did that, that is when he started rising up, because he started making decisions and he started speaking with incredible wisdom that left people coming back for more. As he gained knowledge through life's experiences, he could take that knowledge and use it with wisdom."

You can read as many books as you like. You can pump your head so full of knowledge from different authors and different theologians and different studies, but unless you have the wisdom of the Lord you are not going anywhere. Your boat has sunk before you have even started. So for the analyticals out there, I am sure I am giving you a bit of a knock, but that is the way it is. If you are to minister, minister from the Spirit, not from your head!

5th Pointer: No Preconceived Ideas

Next, do not come to a person with preconceived ideas. Nobody likes to be put in a box. Nobody likes to be put in a cookie cutter and made to think that they are the same as everybody else. And you know what? The Lord did not create us that way either. He made us individuals. He made each of us different and special. So when you are coming to minister an interpretation to someone, they have an interpretation that is suited to them. When interpreting internal dreams, every person has different emotions, they have different hobbyhorses and they have different needs and desires. What worked for the first person you ministered to is not going to work for the next.

I have seen this so much when I have been doing the evaluations for our Fivefold Ministry Schools. I will receive two evaluations from two individuals and each of them will say practically the same things. Their answers will pretty much be the same. However somehow, when I minister to the first person the Lord will give me a strong word of correction and say, "You need to deal with this and this and this in your life." For the other person who said practically the exact same thing, the revelation will come and will say, "You are doing well. The Lord is going to raise you to a higher level. You're excelling. Go for it!"

Now, if you had to try and figure that out with your mind, it would not make much sense. That is because there are no set rules. What applies to one person does not apply to the next. And if you are going to answer the same person the same way for each question, you are going to miss it, because every single one of us is different. That is one of the greatest things that you are going to come across.

You will get those people who just defy the rules. If you set in stone that this symbol means this for all people, just around the corner there is somebody who is going to come and defy that rule, just to get at you. You are then going to have to reevaluate the way you have seen everything and the way you have thought everything to be, because suddenly they do not fit inside your mold.

So if you are the kind of person who likes to get yourself into a rut, if you plan on ministering to others expect to have that rut crushed frequently. Expect to have your direction changed frequently, because for as often as you get yourself into a rut the Holy Spirit is going to work that you are shaken out of it. So prepare yourself for change now, because change is the middle name for Holy Spirit!

6th Pointer: Do Not Use as a Whip

The last point to remember when you come to minister is that the word of revelation you receive is not to be used as a whip to promote your own ideas. The Word of God is never to be used as a whip. The soldiers whipped Jesus as a form of punishment. Jesus never takes a whip in His hands and beats His Bride. And if you are to be a gift to the Body of Christ you are not to be wielding that whip to them either.

I have seen this all too often, where people have come to submit their dreams and revelations to someone. And so this prophet or individual will take that dream and turn it around in such a way that they can use the revelation as a whip against that person, to get them back for something that they are mad about. They may have had bitterness concerning that person. They may dislike some of what this person believes. So what you will have is a revelation being used as a strong correction and a whip to cut down and destroy and break down. That is not the Spirit of God.

We already saw in deception how our God is not one who is forceful, but is gentle and loving, and He woos. That is the attitude that we are to have when are ministering to His Body. Don't wield the whip. The root of all ministry is love. God is love, and that goes right back to keeping that inner stream clear. Make sure that before you sit down to interpret any revelation, there is no bitterness or jealousy, pride or malice in your heart towards anyone. Because if there is, when you sit down to give that revelation, your revelation will be colored by that malice or jealousy or pride or bitterness, and you will not be speaking for the Lord.

That means you stand before God convicted. That means you have to stand before Him and say, "Lord, I didn't speak for You. I spoke out of my own malice and bitterness." Do you have the guts to stand up in front of the Lord and say, "I didn't represent You correctly. I didn't show You as You really are." Are you prepared to take that weight on your shoulders? Because that is the weight you put on your shoulders when you stand up to minister. We are supposed to be representing the Lord Jesus Christ. Make sure that when you are giving an interpretation you are representing the Lord Jesus

Christ, and that you are not representing your own agendas, your own doctrines, or your own ideas.

The minute you step out of the love of the Lord, that is the minute you fall into deception, and it is the minute that the fruit that you are putting into others will go rotten. Nobody likes rotten fruit, let's be honest.

Interpreting Internal Dreams

7 If you abide in Me, and My words abide in you, you will ask what you desire, and it shall be done for you.

8 By this My Father is glorified, that you bear much fruit; so you will be My disciples.

~ John 15:7-8

Chapter 20 – Interpreting Internal Dreams

Let's start looking at internal dreams. You already have an idea of how to interpret your internal dream. And when you are coming to interpret an internal dream of another it is very similar. This is not like the prophetic ministry where the less you know about somebody the better, because then you can get revelation. No, in an internal dream all the characters and objects are symbolic of the person. It is vital that you have some background information concerning the person you are ministering to, because if you do not have that information, you are going to misrepresent the characters. Then what is going to happen is you will give them an interpretation that is way off beam.

Gather Information

I have seen misinterpretation in this arena all too often. Somebody thinks that because the father in this dream represents the Lord, therefore he must represent the Lord in all internal dreams. Then somebody has a dream and says, "I dreamt my father was beating me up." That person will say, "Aha, that's what it means. The Lord is beating you up. You've been a bad boy. Sort yourself out!"

I do not think so! In that case the father does not represent the Lord, because that is not the nature of our

Father. So it is very important that you get a bit of background information on the person whose dream you are interpreting.

Gender

The first bit of information you will need to find out is what their gender is. Are they male, are they female? Are they a guy or a girl? This is very important, because in an internal dream the symbols and objects will be very gender-related, as we have already discussed in another chapter.

Race or Culture

The next thing you will need to understand is their race or culture. This is something that is very important, because something that is common to your race is not common to another. We have also dealt with this in the previous chapters.

Characters, Objects and Animals

The third point that you will need to question the person on is the relationship with the characters in their dreams. This one is very important. If somebody is dreaming of their mother or their spouse or their children or their friend, whoever the character is they need to give you the kind of relationship they have with that person. If the person in their dream is somebody famous that they do not personally know, then you must ask them how they see this person. Do they see this person in a positive light? Do they look up to this person? Do they admire this person? Or do they look down on this person and see him or her as a heretic? It is very important that you know the relationship that person has with the characters that have been displayed in their dreams.

There will often be times where there will be a male or female character in their dream that they do not know at all. This would go under the male and female characters that we have already discussed – the anima and the animus – your male or female side. So keep your eyes open for that one, because those two characters are very common in internal dreams.

When somebody dreams of objects or animals it is also very important to know if they are familiar with that object. If they are dreaming about a car or a vase or a desk or whatever the object is, are they familiar with this object? Is this an object that they use now? What is their relationship, if you will, with this object? What is their familiarity with it? Because whatever their attitude is to this object, it is going to give you an insight of what that object represents in their dream. If they are not familiar with it, then the dream could very well be an internal prophetic dream.

It is the same with animals. You need to know what the animal represents. There was a time when one lady was submitting her dreams to me and she used to dream about her cats. It turned out that this particular woman could not have any children, so her cats were really her children. They were her babies because she could not fall pregnant. So immediately in her dream, when she dreamt about cats I knew that they were speaking of her ministry, those things that she had birthed and were her responsibility. This is because in real life those cats were her children.

However, there is somebody else who cannot stand cats, detests cats, and cannot bear to be in the same room as a cat! Now if he had to dream about such a cat the last thing I would advise was that it was his ministry. I would likely say that cat was the devil incarnate, because he had such a dislike for the animal. So it is very imperative that you find out first the relationship between the person and the animal, so that you can get a clear interpretation.

Interpreting Internal Prophetic Dreams

Now, when you come to the internal prophetic dream, the rules change a little, because now you have a mixture happening. You have a mixture between the common and the uncommon. What you will often find in an internal prophetic dream is that some of the symbols are familiar to the person, but yet some of the objects and symbols are not. This is the first telltale sign that the dream is actually internally prophetic and not just a straight internal dream, when some of the objects and symbols in the dream are totally unfamiliar to the person who is having the dream.

So if you are coming to interpret a dream for somebody, for some of the objects they can clearly say, "I understand and I have a relationship with this person in the dream and I understand this object. This object, though, I've never seen and this object is not familiar to me." If there is an object that is out of place in the dream, you know that you are dealing with an internal prophetic dream, which means that it is relating to their future.

Sort it Out

So what you have to do when you are faced with such a dream, is to do a little bit of sorting. You will need to sort out those symbols that are common to the person and you will need to sort out those symbols that are not so common to them. That is because the symbols that are common you can interpret as an internal dream, but the symbols that are uncommon you have to go to the Word about. This is where the revelation within you steps in, and you can start giving them direction for the future.

Examples

I have taken a few examples for you here and I am going to share them with you. Then I will take them and break them down piece by piece. I want you to see if you can apply the principles to the dreams yourself, before I give you the answers. Then after we have broken it down and had a good look at the characters and the kind of dream it is, I will give the full interpretation that I gave this person. Each of these cases are real cases which I responded to publicly, mostly submitted by the students in our Fivefold Ministry Schools.

"White Cadillac"

The first dream is a good example of one that produced hope.

"I was working for a very large company. A coworker went with me to watch my white Cadillac get repossessed. I had a white Cadillac in 1993 that was repossessed a few months before I was saved. We kept waiting for them to take the car, and then my husband came along with the car and I asked him why he had the car. He said that he took care of it, and that I could keep it. I noticed that the front passenger side tire was not a full-sized tire, but one of those really small donut tires that they used for spares, yet my husband told me to go ahead and get in and drive the car.

I was hesitant, because I just did not feel like the car belonged to me. I did get in the driver's seat, but was careful not to become too attached to it for fear that the car would either break down because of the tire, or that it may be taken away from me again. I noticed that the interior was cloth instead of leather. End of dream."

Personal Details:

EXAMPLE OF: Hope

SEX: Female

RACE: American

RELATIONSHIP WITH CHARACTERS: On questioning discovered relationship with spouse as not positive.

FAMILIAR OBJECTS: Cadillac was a familiar object. Was repossessed a few months before she was saved. It was an object that related to the past and also before salvation.

Breakdown of the Dream:

This is a clear internal dream. She is familiar with all the symbols and has given us a bit of history on the Cadillac. You can see that it is very much an internal dream, because she was active and a participant in this dream.

When I questioned her a bit, this is what I got. She was obviously female, American in race, and the only thing that confused me in coming to interpret this dream is that I did not have an idea of her relationship with her husband. Now, this is a very good example of what I shared earlier about knowing the relationship with the husband. If she had had a positive and a good relationship with her husband, I would say that the Holy Spirit was leading her to go back and that she must start back at basics. Her husband would have represented the Lord and he would have been leading her.

However, if she had a negative relationship with her husband, that would change the entire meaning. It would mean then that she is somehow being forced to go back, and that her husband represents pressure and the flesh, and that she was being pressured into a position where she should not be going. With that in mind I asked her, and it turned out that she actually had a negative relationship with her husband. So in this case, the husband in her dream did not have a positive connotation at all.

If you look at the object, which is the Cadillac car, she was familiar with this object, denoting an internal dream. In fact this object had been repossessed a few months before she was saved. That also gave me a bit of a hint as to what this object meant to her and where it panned out in the whole dream.

So if I take the points that we used in straight internal dream interpretation, the dream was internal. Upon reading it, the spirit of the dream or the first gut feel if you will that I had concerning this dream was negative. I did not feel that here being pressured into that situation was a good thing, although I had to question her on her husband to make doubly sure. My initial reaction was, "This is not of God." It was a negative impression.

The characters in her dream were her husband. In this case it had a negative connotation. He spoke of the temptation and the pressure that was being put on her to conform.

The object was the car, and immediately I identified that the car was past ministry, very likely the ministry that she had started out with just at salvation, but it had been repossessed. The Lord had taken it away. She had moved on to better things. But here in this dream she was being pushed back into that same mold again.

Are you starting to see the picture unravel? Are you starting to see what exactly has been happening in her life? Here is a breakdown of the dream as you would have done it, followed by my final interpretation. Let's see how right you were!

My Interpretation:

DREAM TYPE: Internal

SPIRIT: Negative undertones

CHARACTERS: Husband in this case speaks of the world and her temptation to conform.

OBJECTS: Car speaks of her past condition. First exposure to ministry. The car is also in a bad condition. Negative connotation

INTERPRETATION: What you have shared is enough for me to identify what your husband represents in your dream. When I read over it my first impression was negative. With your husband insisting you drive the car, I had to identify if he represented a positive or a negative picture before clarifying the interpretation. It would seem to me that you are being pressured at this time, firstly to delve into past issues and then also into taking on ministry responsibilities, perhaps even a ministry function that is not of the Lord.

The car is a clear representation of your past and what you have come out of, yet in your dream you are being pressured to go back into it. The Lord never forces His will, and so this is the first indication that the direction you are being pressured into at this time is a deception from the enemy.

You were correct in feeling that the car did not belong to you, because it had been put behind you. I sense accusation and I would say your husband represents sin of the flesh. He is the owner of the car. You are being forced to go back and address issues of your past sin which have been dealt with and repossessed by the Spirit of God. Do not allow the enemy to accuse you any longer and do not feel you have to settle for second best. It is time to put the past behind you and rise up now. Set your face forward and claim in faith the fullness that the Lord has for you.

I am also inclined to feel that the Lord would move you into a new ministry function, and the old function you operated in before has now become obsolete in the work that the Lord has for you. You are to move to a new level. Leave the old car behind. It cannot even ride properly because of the bad wheel. In addition, it is in the shade and not in the light of Jesus. It is time to move on. Shake off the accusation, responsibility, obligations of the past and your old ministry abilities and step into the newness of everything the Lord has for you.

Wrapping it Up:

Can you see how I used that interpretation as an opportunity to speak out and minister and motivate her hope? When she posted that, she was feeling down and discouraged, and as I ministered the interpretation my goal was to lift her up and to give her hope, set her eyes on the correct picture that she should be aiming for, putting the old behind her. That is what you should be doing in interpretation - not just giving people symbols and meanings, but actually using it as a ministry to encourage them and to lift them up and motivate them onto the next thing that the Lord has for them.

"Fish in Hand"

Let's go on to the next dream. I used here a good example of penitence.

"I was going to attend a church conference service, one being held at our church in the coming weeks. As I was going in, one choir member said to the other that she needed a robe and could she wear hers.

Then the scene changed to me walking outside the church with this lady whose daughter I teach at school. We seemed to be in a garden and there were two beautiful flowers that were in full bloom. I said to the lady, "These are pretty," and she said, "Don't touch them, because you'll get very sick like my daughter, and it lasts for a year." Then she walked away.

I went to the flowers to get a closer look and I knocked the flower over and noticed that it was not well rooted in the ground at all. Then I went to the other one beside it, and it was rooted, because I had to pick up a stick to dig in the ground in order to get it up. Finally it came up, but with this flower I looked to see what was in the dirt. It was a flounder fish and a hand from below the elbow down. They did not look scary, but to be very moist. So with the stick I picked the fish and hand up and threw it on the ground."

Personal Details:

> **EXAMPLE OF:** Penitence
>
> **SEX:** Female
>
> **RACE:** American
>
> **RELATIONSHIP WITH CHARACTERS:** Friendly terms
>
> **FAMILIAR OBJECTS:** Choir member, church and friend
>
> **UNFAMILIAR OBJECTS:** Fish, hand and deadly flower

Breakdown of the Dream:

The first time you read the dream it sounds way out. You think, "I haven't a clue what this woman is talking about!" Can you see how there are objects that are familiar to her and there are objects that are not so familiar to her? This indicates a very clear internal prophetic dream.

Now, when somebody presents you with a dream that seems so way out, do not panic! Sort the objects and characters out. Sort those things out that are common and familiar and then sort out those things that are not so familiar. When you can do that, you will start making sense of the dream.

Let's take a quick look at this person and what we know about the characters and objects.

Firstly, we know that she is a woman. I know that she is American. The relationship with the characters – she is on friendly terms with the lady and the daughter. She teaches the daughter. They are on good platonic terms.

The objects – there are two kinds. There are the familiar objects, the choir member, the church and the friend. The unfamiliar symbols, the fish in the hand and the deadly flower. Those three are the ones that likely confused you.

The dream is internal prophetic. The spirit on the dream – I sensed it to be negative. When I first read it the feeling I felt deep inside was, "Uh oh, no." That is the feeling I got. It was very negative.

When you look at the characters, the choir and the woman whose daughter she teaches speak of ministry. They are in a church environment. She teaches this woman's daughter. It speaks of ministry and what she has been ministering with up until now.

The objects also speak of ministry. The choir robe, the mantle, something that you wear. The flower speaks of fruit. For the unfamiliar objects I went to the Word and did a little bit of digging, and the flower always speaks of fruit; the fruit of those things we bear; the fruit of those things which we pour into others.

The fish in the hand causing death has a negative connotation. What I did for the fish in the hand is I did a little bit of searching in the Word. There is a Scripture that I found. But so far, we are getting a negative impression here. Firstly, her ministry. She is wearing a robe that she asked for from somebody else. This is the first thing that something is wrong. She is wearing a robe that is not her own.

Secondly, these flowers that are so brilliant are causing people to be sick. This does not have a good connotation at all. The fact that it made the woman's daughter sick who she teaches, would show that the fruit being born in those whom she is teaching is making them sick. There is something wrong with the fruit. And when we do a little digging below the surface we find the root of her problem, and that is the fish in hand.

Are you starting to get a picture yet? If you have a Bible concordance do a bit of looking up on fish and hand and see what you come up with. Here is the breakdown along with my final interpretation.

My Interpretation:

> **DREAM TYPE:** Internal Prophetic
>
> **SPIRIT:** Negative
>
> **CHARACTERS:** Choir and woman speak of ministry.
>
> **OBJECTS:** Speaks of ministry. The flower speaks of her fruit (her fruit is deadly – something is wrong). Fish and hand causing the death. Look to the Word for revelation of these objects.

INTERPRETATION: Your dream is clearly an internal prophetic one. In other words, it is directly related to you and it has a future orientation with regards to your ministry. Let's take a look at the choir girl asking for the other's robe. The robe speaks of a ministry mantle. Have you perhaps been trying to wear a mantle that was not your own at the time of this dream? Perhaps you have been operating in a ministry that is not really what you were called to operate in.

If you take a further look at your dream there are some symbols in it that do not relate to everyday life. When this happens, you need to look to the Word for an interpretation. A fish in hand is not something you would find in everyday life, so I used the Fivefold Ministry Bible and did a search on hand and fish and this is what I came up with.

> *"Why, when I came, was there no man? Why, when I called, was there none to answer? Is My hand shortened at all that it cannot redeem? Or have I no power to deliver? Indeed with My rebuke I dry up the sea, I make the rivers a wilderness; Their fish stink because there is no water, and die of thirst."*
>
> *~ Isaiah 50:2*

There seems to be something wrong in your ministry. The fruit, which are the flowers, are deadly and are not giving the pleasure and the life that flowers usually bring. However, the exciting part is that the Holy Spirit is going to give you revelation with regards to this problem. Perhaps you have been facing a death in your ministry lately and things have not gone quite as you planned. There is a reason for this. At the root of your problem there is no water. Water epitomizes the anointing of the Spirit. Perhaps you have stepped out of the will of God in your life. Has there been a direction the Lord has been leading you in lately that you have ignored? If this is the case, then you need to find where you missed it and get back on the right path.

Whichever way you look at it, there is something wrong with the fruit. It is bringing death and not life. I sense, though, that with you digging through the soil and seeing the root of evil, that the Lord is about to reveal to you clearly the source of your fruit going bad. My advice to you is to seek the Lord concerning the path He has for you and step into His will for your life. As you do this those deadly fruits will be rooted up and you will then be able to begin on a new road of victory and authority in the spiritual realm.

Wrapping It Up

I received a very positive feedback from this dream and it was confirmed that the person in question had been operating in a ministry that was not her calling. But you see how a dream that seems so way out and so impossible to interpret, if you just take it and break it down a bit and wait on the Lord for a bit of revelation, He will always come up with the goods.

"Tornadoes"

The third example I have here is a good one of preservation and how we stand against the enemy in our Christian walk. The dream is called Tornadoes. She said she had two dreams.

First Dream...

"My husband and I were standing together. As we were standing there tornadoes of all sizes and shapes, from little ones just starting to ones that resemble an F5 are all around us. They are not coming near us, but they are all around us."

Second Dream...

"Our whole family is standing on a bluff overlooking I think the Southwest somewhere. We are all together and we see about seven tornadoes all across from us. They start coming towards us, one at a time. As they reach us they just turn into a slight breeze. It is as if they had been thrown towards us, the entire family, not just me and the two children."

Personal Details:

EXAMPLE OF: Preservation

SEX: Female

RACE: American

FAMILIAR OBJECTS: Tornadoes

Breakdown of the Dream:

What do we have here? The gender was a female. The race and culture was very important here. She was American. You may ask why that was so important. Simply because she knows what a tornado is. Americans might know what a tornado is, but where I come from in South Africa I have never seen one anywhere near me. I do not know so much what a tornado is or what one looks like, other than what I have seen on TV. It is not something that we have had to deal with. It is not a part of our lives or a part of where we come from. But in this instance she has obviously had much experience with tornadoes, cyclones, hurricanes and that sort of thing. It is because it is common in the region where she lives.

That would have been something totally unfamiliar to me. If I had dreamt about tornadoes I would likely have looked in the Word to get clear symbols, because it is not something I am familiar with. It is not something that I grew up with; it is not a template. But in this case it is a template for her. It is part of what she grew up in and it is part of her culture.

The dream is clearly internal. All the symbols are common to her. The spirit is obviously negative. It pictures attack, things coming at them. The characters in her dream are her husband and her children, her husband representing the Lord, standing by her side. The tornado speaks of destruction and the works of the enemy, yet somehow the tornado did not touch them. Her children represent her ministry that stood by her side, also untouched by the attack.

I am sure that you by now have a very clear interpretation. Here is the breakdown and interpretation in a nutshell.

My Interpretation:

    DREAM TYPE: Internal

SPIRIT: Negative, leading to positive

CHARACTERS: Husband and children. Husband speaks of the Lord. Children speak of her ministry.

OBJECTS: Tornado speaks of destruction, works of the enemy, yet they did not cause real damage!

INTERPRETATION: This dream is clearly an internal dream. Have you been facing personal attack lately – attack to your ministry and attack to your personal life? These attacks have not destroyed you. However, I do sense that they have perhaps worn you down. Without knowing your personal information I am simply going by what I sense in the Spirit. The enemy has been attacking you, and I would like to suggest that you listen to the *Strategies of War* Mp3 Series. The enemy has an open door in your life, one that you need to identify and close on him. The Lord is protecting you, but if the enemy has license he will make full use of that license.

Your husband speaks of the Lord, and you can be encouraged that no matter what you are going through or will go through, the Lord will never leave your side and your ministry will remain protected under His wings.

"Convertible"

Let's go on to our last example. The fourth example gives a lovely portrayal of faith and hope. I have called this dream "Convertible."

"I was wandering about in this dream and I was at a fairly large church in the front row with my husband and a friend. The people on stage noticed me and called me out and told me that they wanted me to go and work for them. In the dream I was serving food.

At the end of the dream my husband and I were leaving the church in a really nice convertible car. There were people working in a field and they all stopped and watched us as we left. I remember feeling like I did not want to be overly noticed as we were leaving."

Personal Details:

EXAMPLE OF: Faith and hope

SEX: Female

RACE: American

CHARACTERS: Husband and church members

OBJECTS: Familiar and unfamiliar

Breakdown of the Dream:

I see symbols and characters here that are familiar to this dreamer, but there are some symbols that are not. The convertible car is not something that she is familiar with. She does not own a convertible car. She has no familiarity or personal attachment to this particular object. So in looking at this dream I sense it is an internal prophetic dream, some of the objects being familiar and some being not so familiar.

Once again the gender is female, and she is an American. The characters that she is familiar with are the husband and the church members. The object she is familiar with is the church, and the unfamiliar objects are obviously the car and her serving the food.

The dream is an internal prophetic dream. When I read this dream the spirit on it was positive. I felt something good inside when I read it. I felt that the Lord was trying to tell her something positive and good. I felt those butterflies in my stomach that said, "This is going to be a good one!"

The characters - her husband speaks of the Lord. The worship leaders and those who were on the stage spoke of the church. The objects that were familiar - the church speaks of her local fellowship where she is right now amongst the believers. The objects that are unfamiliar to her are:

a. The food. Food always speaks of ministering the Word in Scriptures.

b.   The convertible car, which more often than not speaks of the vehicle for your ministry, and this, was a convertible car, so we are looking at a ministry that has been promoted.

Are you starting to get a picture? She was sitting in the front row. She was called out by the church leadership. She served food and then she drove off in a convertible car. Can you see a progression happening here? Let's look at the breakdown and final interpretation.

My Interpretation:

DREAM TYPE: Internal Prophetic

SPIRIT: Positive

CHARACTERS: Husband speaks of the Lord. Worship leaders speak of the church

FAMILIAR OBJECTS: The church, which speaks of her local fellowship with believers.

UNFAMILIAR OBJECTS: Food, which speaks of ministering the Word. The convertible car, which speaks of a promotion in ministry.

INTERPRETATION: This dream is clearly an internal prophetic one. In other words, it concerns you and has a future orientation. You begin this dream by sitting in your church. Now, I do not know much about you, so I am going by the Spirit. Perhaps right now you might feel that you are not progressing sitting on the front pew. However, in your dream those in your church have called you to help. This indicates that the Lord is going to open the way for you to get involved in the local church. You will serve food and feed those under your care. This I believe will be a preparation for a higher calling. Already the Lord has pushed you forward. You are sitting in the front row and even though you may not feel like it, He sees you. He sees that you are ready to become active now in the work.

Now, later on in the dream, you leave the church in a new car. This speaks of promotion to one of the fivefold ministry offices. But, the preparation will come first and you will learn to be a servant first. The time will come after that preparation that you will be led out of the local church and into a calling that will embrace the universal Body of Christ.

If this sounds a bit strange to you do not feel concerned. As I see it, this is a very normal process of one with a calling, being prepared and trained by the Holy Spirit. I would like to invite you to check out our various Schools to find out from the Lord which of the fivefold ministries you are called to. When you know your calling then you will have a clearer picture. We have put together a complete Fivefold Ministry Evaluation, called 'Signs of the Fivefold Ministry', which is very extensive and will give you a clear picture of what you are called to do. In the meantime, rest assured that the Lord has all in hand. Your husband represents the Lord Jesus in your dreams, and as he has been with you throughout your dream, so will the Lord Jesus be with you throughout this process.

Wrapping It Up:

I could see very clearly in this dream that this particular person was in preparation for one of the fivefold ministries. The signs were so clear. Firstly, she was sitting in obscurity doing nothing, then the Lord edged her up to the front pew. After this she was called out to serve, and then she left the church in a promoted ministry, to go out 'there', into the field to the Body Universal.

Let it Flow

As you come to sit down and you pull the characters apart as I have shown you, sit down if you have the dream on paper and journal the interpretation. Write what comes out of your spirit. Do not write what comes out of your head. As you do this it will begin to flow easier and you will find things starting to pop out as you are writing, that you did not think of before. As you do that, this is when the revelation really starts coming and really starts getting exciting. Then that wisdom is going to start flowing and you are going to start giving people direction for their lives.

I can tell you that there is no greater satisfaction in the world than sharing with somebody, giving them an interpretation and encouragement and actually seeing it mean something; seeing it change their lives; seeing it change the direction in their lives and seeing it bear fruit in their lives.

If you would tap that wisdom that is within you and as you continue to pour that wisdom out in others, others are going to start looking to you more and more. And the more they look to you, the more that wisdom will pour out, and then there is no stopping it. You will be a yielded vessel to the Lord. And as you let it flow it will keep on flowing and continue flowing at a greater capacity.

So start where you are. Start with the one dream then the two dreams and before you know it, you are going to have a whole torrent to deal with. And whatever you do, do it to bear fruit in others, and do it with love, representing the Lord Jesus Christ.

CHAPTER **21**

Revelation and Discernment

2 Then the Lord answered me and said: "Write the vision and make it plain on tablets, that he may run who reads it.

3 For the vision is yet for an appointed time; but at the end it will speak, and it will not lie. Though it tarries, wait for it; because it will surely come, It will not tarry,

~ Habbakuk 2:2-3

Chapter 21 —Revelation and Discernment

Failure in Interpretations

In this chapter we will be looking at spiritual revelation and discernment, particularly when coming to the interpretation and receiving revelation through visions. We have discussed some of the symbols and we have discussed how to receive a vision, but now comes the most vital part of receiving revelation, and that is the interpretation of that revelation.

If there is one thing that I have seen people fail at time and time again in receiving visions, it is not by any means their revelation, but rather their interpretation of that revelation. Even in training the prophets in our Prophetic School, the correction that we have had to take them through time and time again has not been the revelation that they received. The revelation they received was not usually the deception. However, it was the way in which they interpreted it that ended up becoming a deception.

Firstly they tried to interpret it using their minds, secondly they did not check the interpretation against the Word, and thirdly they did not test the spirit of the interpretation against the gift of discerning of spirits. All three of these are factors that need to be taken into account when coming to interpret your own visions and the visions given to you by others.

I will be taking you through some basic guidelines on how to apply these three principles and also how to give some insight to others on their revelations. As I was pondering how to deal with this I said to the Lord, "Lord, why haven't you given me a clearer cut strategy and pattern for people to know exactly how to interpret their visions step by step like I received for dreams?"

When coming to interpret an internal dream, I can give it to you step by step and you could probably follow a lot of the interpretation with the knowledge you have accumulated through this book. But somehow when coming to interpret visions, I did not receive the same insight and I said, "Lord, why aren't You showing me how to explain to people how to interpret their visions?"

Spiritual Discernment

He answered me very simply. He said to me, "How can you possibly put knowledge in the mind of one to interpret something that is spiritual? How can you teach man in his mind how to interpret something that comes from the everlasting Father that comes from the heavenly realm?"

I have discussed how the mind and the soulish man cannot comprehend the things of the Spirit. So before we proceed, have this very clearly in your mind, that you cannot interpret visions without that revelation coming from the Word and from your spirit. It is impossible to have an understanding of visions without receiving the revelation along with that vision, because these matters are spiritually discerned.

So what I will be discussing in this chapter is not so much how to interpret a vision, but how to discern for yourself and how to sense from your own spirit how to receive the interpretation. When it comes to visions there is no clear-cut 'A-B-C' of vision interpretation, because each revelation will come directly to you from the Spirit of the Lord, and you will receive that revelation, if you know how to look out for that interpretation.

Dark Sayings

Hosea 12:10 says:

> *"I have also spoken by the prophets, and have multiplied visions; I have given symbols through the witness of the prophets."*

We have looked quite extensively at dark sayings, at parables, at symbolism, and right through the Word you will find those sayings said over and over again – visions, dark saying, visions upon the bed, parables. Jesus, when He walked the earth continually spoke in parables. He spoke in pictures, because that is the way humans think. We think in pictures. We are very visual creatures. It is the way that God has created us.

So even now, by this stage in the book, you have started to see visions. You have started to have dreams, and the well within you has begun to bubble up. But all these dreams and visions you have been receiving will be in dark sayings. They will be in parables or in symbolism. This is how the Lord begins to talk with you. And as you progress through those dark sayings, you go on to where the Lord spoke of Moses and He says, "With my prophets I spoke in dark sayings, but not with my servant Moses. With him I spoke face to face."

Know Him Face to Face

In learning to interpret dreams and visions, that is your ultimate goal - to get to the place in your spiritual walk where you are speaking to the Lord face to face. Where it is no longer dark sayings and hidden gestures and parables, but where He is talking to you straight like Jesus spoke to His disciples straight on the night of the last supper.

Perhaps you have been moving in prophetic circles. Perhaps you have had this feeling within that the Lord is directing you towards the Prophetic Ministry. If this is the case, then this chapter is definitely for you, because it will encourage you to let that gift flow from within. However do not think that this is just for the prophet. A believer, perhaps functioning as a teacher, evangelist or pastor can see dreams and visions and interpret them. It is a gift of the Spirit. And although prophets do function in it more than most, every believer can have visions and every believer can use the wisdom of the Spirit to interpret that revelation.

Different Rules

Dark sayings are the secret language of God, and we have looked at that extensively. If you tap into those dark sayings you can understand what the Lord is saying to you at any time. But now, as we have looked at dream interpretation and in looking at visions, the tendency is for you to take what you learned in dreams and to apply them to visions when interpreting them. This is the number one mistake you can make, because when you come to interpret visions, the same set of rules do not apply in interpretation. The same rules apply to receiving the revelation, but not to interpreting the revelation.

In dreams we start looking for internal symbols that relate to the person. We start looking for your templates, your race, your culture, your gender, things that apply to you. But when you receive revelation from the Spirit, these things no longer apply, because the Spirit speaks with a universal language, and that universal language is Genesis to Revelation. So if ever you want to learn the language of God that would be a good book to start with. The Lord will always speak through His Word and His revelation will always back up His Word, and His Word will always back up His revelation. The two go hand in hand.

Balancing Spirit and Word

Do not think that you can be all Spirit and no Word, and do not think that you can be all Word and no Spirit, because either side of the balance you are lacking. So if you have been running headlong and getting revelation, but have not actually stopped to glean the truth from the Word, you are headed straight for deception, because without the Word to balance you, you will go way off. It is the interpretation that many fail at. It is not the revelation that is the difficult part. The difficult part is interpreting that revelation. And if your feet are not solidly grounded on the Word of God, your interpretation will go way off beam, and you will lead people astray.

I may really emphasize this a lot, but that is because I have seen it so much in training the prophets. Unfortunately they tend to concentrate a lot on the spiritual realm, so much so that they neglect the Word. The minute they do that, they fall headlong into deception and then cannot understand how they ended up there. The Word is our meter. It meters what comes out of our spirits. If you want to know how to interpret, your 'A-B-C' and 'step 1-2-3' is to get into the Word of God. Soak in it, meditate on it and know it, because when you know it, then the interpretations will fall into place for you. You will not even have to think twice. They will make perfect sense with the revelation that the Lord has given to you.

Internal and External Visions

Now just as we had internal and external dreams, the same applies also to visions. When you receive revelation, there are times when you will be receiving revelation for yourself, which is an internal vision, and there will be times when you will receive revelation on behalf of another, which would be an external vision. You need to be able to discern the difference between the two, because it is so common to mistake revelations you receive for yourself and think they are for somebody else, and vice versa.

So, when coming to interpret a vision, there is one very important thing you need to ask the person who had the vision and that is, "Where and when did you receive this vision?" Did they receive this vision in church doing praise and worship? Did they receive it during intercession? Did they receive it while they were praying on their own in their room? Did they have it while they were lying on their bed, or did they have it while they were ministering to somebody else?

That is the only information you need to receive from somebody when interpreting their vision for them. Where and when did they receive that vision? What were the circumstances that surrounded that vision? The minute you know what those circumstances were, you know where to aim that interpretation, whether it should be aimed directly at the person, or whether it is external and must therefore be aimed at those they saw in the vision.

Paths of Revelation

How do you discern between the two? The Lord gave me revelation and He said to me, "The Spirit will speak in the same direction as what is in your mind." He showed it to me in the Spirit like this. I saw in the spiritual realm many different 'paths of revelation', if you will. As I got myself on one path I started walking on that one path. As I walked along that path I picked up all the pieces of revelation that were on that specific path for that specific time. Then the Lord led me to Romans 8:27 which says:

"And he that searches the hearts knows what the mind of the Spirit [is], because he makes intercession for the saints according to [the will of] God."

When you come into prayer, whether it is on your own behalf or on behalf of somebody else, you are entering into the mind of the Spirit. That is the realm that you are moving into now. And just like your mind can only comprehend one thought after another, so in the spiritual realm it will only comprehend one vision after another. It is like one single stream coming up from your spirit, into your mind and out again. You cannot have five streams gushing at the same time.

So if you are in intercession on your own behalf, perhaps for a physical need or a financial need, perhaps for a healing need, you will receive revelation with regard to what you are praying for. Why? It is because that is the mind of the Spirit - the path of the Spirit that you are on. The path you are walking concerns revelation for yourself, for your physical being or financial wellbeing, whichever the case may be. So every revelation you receive in that state of mind is directly related to your prayer.

Now maybe you are praying for somebody else. Perhaps they have come to you for a need with the laying on of hands and you are praying. Now the mind of the Spirit is directed towards that person. The path that you are walking on is now directly related to them and their needs. Every revelation you receive will therefore be according to their need. What you see will not be internal. It will be external. The interpretation will be for them. So you will take the revelation you receive and you will not hold them in your heart, but you will share it with that person, because the Spirit is giving you that revelation for you to specifically share with them.

If you start thinking about this it makes sense, especially if you have been moving a lot in visions. In praise and worship you will see the praise and worship angels in the church. Why? Because that is the mind of the Spirit you are in at that moment. You are in the spiritual realm and on the path of praise and worship in your local congregation. So the revelation that will come to your mind will be along that path and along that direction.

This is why it is vital, when interpreting a vision, that you know the circumstances. Try and identify the mind of the Spirit for that specific time, and you will then know the will of God, and will be able to minister the answer to that need and for that specific time.

Example of Visions

I would like to share an example here from a lady who was interceding for us at one time. There came a bit of a confusion about the revelation she received, because as she was interceding she started coming into warfare and she saw a huge serpent, ready to strike. She entered into warfare on our behalf came against it, and she dealt with it, and the Lord revealed that there had actually been an attack of deception amongst the students. As she interceded on our behalf she received the revelation that deception was in the camp. She stood against it and averted the attack of the enemy.

Once she had finished her time of intercession she went to bed, and as she lay down on her bed she received a revelation and saw a vision of a native woman bent over and praying over rosary beads. Now, because she had been praying for us in intercession, she automatically connected that vision she received on her bed with the revelation that she received in intercession and felt that perhaps that vision applied to the ministry as well. But somehow she could not understand how it applied, so she came and shared it with us. We could then take that revelation and I could see very clearly what was happening.

In intercession she was in the mind of the Spirit for our ministry, so all the revelations she received during that time were for the ministry and were directly related to us. But then her time of intercession and external revelation ended and she went to bed to go and sleep.

As she was there in her own room, not doing anything in particular she again saw this vision.

Now, the second vision she had of the native girl was an internal vision. It related to her personally. It did not relate to the ministry. Can you see how the change in circumstances and the change in the mind of the Spirit altered the internal and external interpretation? As it turned out, this vision she saw was directly related to a generational bondage that her husband was in.

She later told me that while she was cleaning out her room she found rosary beads in a chest that she had forgotten about. They were in her bedroom and were bringing a curse into their home. So the Lord clarified very clearly that the native woman she saw with the rosary beads was a warning for her. The Lord was trying to show her that there was an open door right there in her room with her husband, where she was. So the Lord unraveled the mystery and showed her exactly what was going on.

Four Pointers for Interpretation

5 A wise man will hear and increase learning,
And a man of understanding will attain wise
counsel,

6 To understand a proverb and an enigma, the
words of the wise and their riddles.

~ Proverbs 1:5-6

Chapter 22 – Four Pointers for Interpretation

There are four points that you need to follow when interpreting a vision. They are very simple points, and you can just keep them at the back of your mind when you are reading or when somebody is sharing a vision with you.

1st Point: Identify Type

Firstly, identify the type of the vision. Ask the person concerning their circumstances. If they were alone during praise and worship or just in prayer, then the revelation is internal and for themselves. If they were interceding for somebody in particular, or if they were ministering to somebody or amongst a particular group of people, then that vision is very likely external. This means that the interpretation and revelation was meant for that group or that person or church that he or she was ministering to.

2nd Point: Discern the Spirit

The next thing you need to do is discern the spirit on the vision. Is the Lord revealing a work of the enemy, or is He revealing a promise or a gift? Does it have a positive or a negative feeling? When I shared the vision that I originally had of the native woman praying over the rosary beads, there was a negative feeling. The vision itself was not necessarily negative, but the spirit on it was negative. It did not feel right.

So you need to test the spirits and know exactly where that vision is at. What was the feeling deep down inside in the pit of your stomach when you had the vision? Did you feel good about it, or was there something that was foreboding about it?

3rd Point: Characters are Real

Next, the characters, particularly in visions are who they really are. Unlike dreams where characters are symbolic, in visions characters are who they really are. If I see my mother or my father or my sister in a vision, they represent my mother or my father or my sister. If I see myself in a vision, I represent me in that vision. It is all pretty simple.

The only time you will see somebody that is not necessarily who they are, is if you are in intercession and the Lord brings a picture to your mind of a group or a specific person that you do not know. This could be in cases where you are interceding 'blindly', for somebody that is on the other side of the world that you have never met before, nor will ever meet. The vision you see there will not likely have the exact features and looks of the person that you are interceding for. Rather, you will receive an impression in your spirit. It has been known, though, for intercessors to see real people, to have interceded for them before having even met.

4th Point: Types are Symbolic

That is the clear-cut difference between visions and dreams that the characters in visions are who they really are. The types, shadows and objects, however, are all obviously symbolic. This is where your dark sayings come in. Symbols are something that you must always interpret with Scripture. Some of them are common sense. We often see very naturalistic symbols in visions where the interpretation is obvious. I have a couple of examples here and you will see what I mean. Some of them are common sense and you do not necessarily have to run to the Word, although if you really had to dig in the Word you will always find something to line up with it.

I think that if Paul knew about television and satellite and radio and all the other modern ways of communication that we have today, he would have very likely spoken about them in the Scriptures. But in that day, there were no such things. So we need to sometimes parallel the modern day equivalent with the Scripture and see exactly what the Spirit is using, because very often the Lord will use things that are familiar to you, so that you can gain understanding from it. I will expand on that more now as we go into the examples.

Examples of Personal Visions

"Prison"

The first example I have chosen really motivated the person to love.

The Vision:

I was ministering to somebody in particular who had really had hurts from the past. They had seemed to come to a plateau in their spiritual walk and could not move past that plateau. As I came to pray with this person I saw what looked like a five year old boy sitting in the corner of a dark room, a prison. He was chained to a wall and he was sitting there in the corner all by himself crying.

As I prayed and interceded on his behalf I saw the Lord Jesus step into the room, bend down and take the chains off. He picked that little boy up and took him out of that dark horrible room, out into the sunshine and into a big meadow where he could just run and play with the other kids. Instead of the tears, he was laughing and joking. He was running around and free.

My Interpretation:

> **VISION TYPE:** Internal
>
> **SPIRIT:** Negative leading to positive
>
> **CHARACTERS:** Person in question having experienced hurts at that age. Jesus, the healer.

NEGATIVE OBJECTS: Prison, chains. They speak of bondage. Self-made prison for protection from further hurt. He had cut off his heart from everyone.

POSITIVE OBJECTS: Sunlight and open meadow speak of liberty and freedom.

ACTION: Cutting the cord.

BREAKDOWN OF THE VISION: If we use the four points I have mentioned above, the interpretation becomes very clear. Firstly, the vision was external. It was not for myself; it was for the person I was ministering to, because that is the mind of the Spirit that I was in at that time.

The character in the vision was the little five year old boy. Upon questioning the person I was ministering to, he related to me that when he was about that age he suffered a lot of rejection from his parents. He felt an outcast, and he felt hurt. He said what he did is he went and sat in the corner of the garden all by himself once and he cried his eyes out. That is what I had seen in the vision. What the Lord was saying is, "At that age, that is when the hurt began. At that age he started building those walls around himself. It was at that age that the chains and shackles were put around his arms and feet, that prevented him from growing up and prevented him from being free."

Let's have a look at the objects. The objects are the prison and chains. If you go to Scripture, both of these speak of bondage. They always speak of your freedom being taken away, of being locked in. Then of course, the light and the meadow afterwards - the light of the Lord and freedom, liberty, joy and peace. Can you see the two pictures?

What had happened is that this little boy, at a very young age, had started building walls around his heart. Because he had been so hurt throughout life he had literally put himself in imprisonment where he said, "If that's what life is like, I'm not going to let anybody hurt me anymore." The problem was he had built so many walls around his heart that even the Lord Jesus could not come in and minister to him. And when it came time for this person to minister to others, he could not do it, because those walls were so strongly around him and those chains bound him so strongly that he could not break free.

In the Spirit I came against those chains and we broke those cords. He asked for forgiveness and he spoke that release and said, "Lord, deal with this issue," and he was set free instantly. There came an immediate change in his ministry, for he could flow out in love and he could stand up and minister in love, and he could receive love for the first time in his life. Suddenly that life that was blocked off from the sunlight just burst open into a beautiful sunlight.

"Stony Heart"

Now here is a similar vision, but this time it has a different emphasis.

The Vision:

I was in prayer and journaling alone in my private time. As I was in prayer and just speaking with the Lord, He showed me a heart encased with stone. As I watched, a little chip was made in the stone of this heart and a light beam shone through it. As the light beam shone through that stone, it started cracking the rest of it. Then as I watched, pieces of stone started falling off this heart, and light radiated where those pieces were chipped away, until that whole heart was radiating with light.

Then I stood back and watched as the light came from the heart and it spread throughout the body and started radiating out from the body. Then wherever that body walked, the light just emanated from it.

Breakdown of the Vision:

I received this vision during my personal time with the Lord. That means that this vision was internal. It was about me specifically. The spirit on the vision was positive. It was healing. Light is always a positive picture.

The object was the heart. What does the heart speak of in Scripture? It speaks of our soul – our mind, emotions and will. It refers to our feelings, the way we think and our mindsets. That is what the heart speaks of in Scripture. Then there was the stone. What does stone speak of in Scripture? It speaks of things that are unmoving and restrictive, blocking in and breaking. A heart covered in stone means a person who cannot love. It reflects a person who is blocked within their own emotion. They have put so much stone around their heart that they no longer know how to love or receive love anymore.

Once again, what caused that? The same thing that caused that little boy to be in prison. It was hurts. With each hurt that I had experienced in life I had added another piece of stone to that heart, where I said, "I won't let him hurt me anymore. I won't let her hurt me anymore." And what had happened? Before I knew it, here I was standing as a wife and mother with this heart encased in stone, and there was nothing I could do about it. No matter how hard I tried to pour out in love or receive it I couldn't. It took the Spirit of the Lord to come into that heart of mine and shatter that stone.

I cannot say that the process was a pleasant one, because cracking and shattering and chipping away are not positive feelings; they are not positive actions. But yet the Lord did it, and He worked in me.

My Interpretation:

VISION TYPE: Internal

SPIRIT: Positive, healing

OBJECTS: Heart was my own. Light was the anointing of the Lord that would break the stone.

ACTION: Lord setting me free from hurts of the past.

INTERPRETATION: The interpretation speaks for itself. The light that came out of that heart was in me all along. So as the Lord took away that restriction, it not only spread out to the rest of my body to where I could receive and give love, but it spread to those around me also. No longer was my emotion contained within me, but I could pour it out freely. And that spirit and that anointing that had been locked up within me all this time because of the mindsets that I had created in my own mind were shattered, and the Lord could begin to use me as a vessel yielded to Him for the first time.

Examples of Student's Visions

I have used a couple of visions here, and every one of them are visions that were submitted to me by my students, so I share them proudly. The interpretation for this particular vision was given by one of our senior students. This example gives direction and hope.

Breaking Ground

"I was in prayer worshipping and praying in tongues, and clear as day in the Spirit with my eyes closed, I saw a nice building, which I knew was a church or something.

Then I saw myself outside of this church. In my vision I was a construction worker. I had a jackhammer that breaks up concrete, and I was breaking the ground, knowing that I was about to build something."

Scriptural Parallels

This is the example that I was referring to earlier when I said; "You can find parallels in the Word for modern day objects." You will see modern objects in vision that you will not necessarily find in the Word. But if you do a little digging for yourself, a jackhammer can very much be related to what is called a rod in Scripture. Paul speaks of the rod of correction. There is often reference to 'the rod that breaks ground'.

So even though a jackhammer is not something that is in Scripture, I can very well parallel that to an object that is in Scripture. In Scriptures they used the rod to break the foundation of an old house, to rebuild it. If they needed to rebuild a house, they did not have jackhammers in those days, so they used to get this rod and literally break the foundation up so that it could be rebuilt. So if I wanted to look up an object in Scripture, I would look up that rod.

Then there is the concrete. Although they did not have concrete in those days, I am sure that they had some pretty heavy stone. If you cannot find the word concrete in Scripture, you are very likely to find stone and rock. There are your parallels.

Breakdown of the Vision:

Okay, let's break this vision down. When did he have this vision? He had it while in prayer, worshipping and praying in tongues. He had this vision in his private time. That means it was internal. The spirit had a positive feeling. It felt good. There was a spirit of change, but somehow it was positive change. It was a nice building. It seemed like he was going somewhere in this vision.

What were the objects? The church, the jackhammer and the concrete. The church, being a building, what does it often represent? It represents yourself, particularly if it is a building that you do not know of. If you see a particular church that you know, then the vision is talking about that specific building. But if you see a church, generally that you do not know about, it can either speak about the church of God, or it can speak about yourself as the temple of the Holy Ghost, as it says in Scripture.

The jackhammer gets back to what I said about the rod breaking the concrete. The concrete is stone, breaking up the foundation. The action of course is him hammering into that concrete.

Interpretation:

> **VISION TYPE:** Internal
>
> **SPIRIT:** Positive, change
>
> **OBJECTS:** Church, speaking of himself. Jackhammer breaks things up. Concrete, a hard unyielding surface being broken up.
>
> **ACTION:** Hammering into the concrete.

FINAL INTERPRETATION: By an AMI Student

Let's look at the final interpretation. This is the revelation that one of our senior students received.

She said, "More than simply priming your pump (she is referring to him speaking in tongues), I feel the Holy Spirit is calling you to become aggressive in your spiritual walk. The verse on my mind is, "Heaven suffers violence and the violent take it by force."

The Lord is calling you to break up the paths of your spiritual walk and heart that have become hardened and sealed off. He is doing this so that the rain of His Spirit might be able to soak into the ground and that He may be able to bring forth a mighty spiritual harvest in and through your life. Do not be dismayed, for the purpose of this is that He may expand and enlarge your spiritual territory. The building (speaking of the church) I believe represents your vessel, which is obviously doing nicely. But there are other areas that the Lord wants to now work on so that you may stretch to the right and to the left and possess the land.

I also see a great excitement in your spirit for the things of God, and I see that you wholeheartedly desire to be the soft, flexible clay in the potter's hand. In fact, I see you going hard with that jackhammer with an absolutely contagious joy, giving it your all. Truly the Lord sees all things and He weighs the motives of a man's heart, and you have been found worthy in His sight!"

Wrapping it Up:

What I loved the most about this interpretation is that the vision itself was not just interpreted, but the interpretation was used as a means of ministry. What I did not share here was the prophecy that Jennifer followed this vision up with, where she encouraged this student to go on for the Lord and to push forward in all that the Lord has for them.

That is really our goal - to use it as a ministry. It is not just to look good and great and intelligent, but to use it as a ministry, to apply the interpretation to the life of the person.

Train

Let's look at our fourth example. This one is an example of the direction and warning that this particular student was about to follow. The vision is called 'Train'.

"There was a train traveling very fast and I was on it, as well as some of my family and a lot of my friends. I could not see beyond the front of the train. Only the friends and family either fell off or decided to get off as the train traveled upward. The path got narrower and it was bumpy and they did not seem to want to continue on."

Breakdown of the Vision:

This person was in the vision. That indicates to me that it is an internal vision. In other words, it was for herself. What is the spirit? The spirit is mixed. Even though the family members were getting off the train, it was still positive. Somehow there was still encouragement in there to keep pushing forward up that hill, even though it did seem to become bumpy. So even though the vision itself may have been negative, the spirit that I sensed on it was actually positive, because it was encouraging the student, "Come on, press forward, keep going. You'll make it."

The objects – the train, the road. What did these speak of? Vehicles often speak of ministry, those things on which you travel, and the road in Scripture speaks of our walk. This road spoke of her ministry. Her ministry was going places, but it was an uphill climb. And if you had to look at that road, it was becoming narrower and bumpier. What happened? As this was happening, her friends and family were jumping off the train. Are you starting to get the picture?

My Interpretation:

>**VISION TYPE:** Internal
>
>**SPIRIT:** Positive
>
>**CHARACTERS:** Family members
>
>**OBJECTS:** Train. Speaks of ministry. Road getting narrow speaks of preparation and ministry walk.
>
>**ACTION:** Riding on train. Moving upwards.

INTERPRETATION: She interpreted this vision very clearly for herself when she said, "I felt that God was saying that I was traveling in a ministry that was of His calling, therefore it was a journey towards Him. However, I wanted everybody with me in this to continue on. I felt very sad that they didn't, but I understood that I had to go on. It became a lonesome journey."

Wrapping it Up:

The Lord was making very clear to her, "I have called you and this is an upward climb, but your friends and family aren't going to carry on with you. But, if you want to continue on this road, there is a reward at the end. You must choose. Are you going to go the long way? Are you going to go on the narrow path, or are you going to get off with them?" But she chose to stick it through with the calling and she is pushing through into all that the Lord has for her.

Travail

The fifth example is one that I think many prophets will identify with, and that is the main reason I included it. It is an example of what happens very often in intercession where prophets go into travail to release into the earth the things that the Lord has for us. It is also a good example of proclamation.

"I was at a church and several brothers and sisters that I fellowship with were present, including our pastor and his wife. I was standing by a chair and all of a sudden I began to go into labor. I could feel in the Spirit that I was very pregnant and that I was getting ready to deliver. I moaned and groaned aloud as I felt myself going through all the stages of labor and delivery. There were others around me who did not understand what was going on. The pastor's wife explained to those observing that I was in travail.

I felt when the membranes broke and got into a squatting position. My body, sweating and trembling from the pain I was in, in my spirit I could see that I was delivering a baby in a field. I began to pant and push. The agony was horrendous, but it was not physical, it was spiritual. I continued in the Spirit until the delivery was complete. My pastor approached me after the delivery to explain what was taking place, but no-one else in the church could discern what was going on. They could not discern that I was bringing forth a child - a spiritual child, a new move of God."

Breakdown of the Vision:

Where did this vision and this whole experience take place? It took place in the context of her church. It was an external vision and an experience that Sarah (not real name) had that particularly related to her church. What was the spirit? It was positive. Birth is always something that is positive.

The characters were the baby and the pregnancy. When you look at those characters in Scripture they always speak of a new life, a new birth, something that is about to enter into the world. A new anointing, a new ministry, a new way of doing things. The object in the vision was the field. What does the field often speak of in Scripture? It speaks of the harvest, the world and being 'out there'. That is what the field speaks of. Then of course, the action was the birthing. Are you starting to see the picture clearly? This was her interpretation, as she saw it.

My Interpretation:

> **VISION TYPE:** External

> **SPIRIT:** Positive

> **CHARACTERS:** Baby, pregnancy. Birth speaks of new life. New ministry, new anointing.

> **OBJECTS:** Field

> **ACTION:** Birthing

INTERPRETATION: Sarah interpreted the experience herself saying, "There is a mighty, powerful move of God on the horizon, unlike anything we have ever seen. I believe the Lord is saying that many in the church will not recognize this new move. Some will even try to stop it. But stay encouraged and continue in intercession. Perseverance in prayer, in spiritual warfare will break down the barriers (the rupturing of the membranes) the enemy is trying to put into place to keep this move of God from coming forth.

I believe this new move will bring about a great harvest of souls (the squatting in the field) and that we have been positioned in Christ (the squatting) to bring this harvest in. There will be much opposition, but the Lord is saying that if we are positioned in Christ, being incessantly prayerful, focused and determined, unmovable, unshaken, that we would gather this mighty harvest. It will be through His Spirit (the Holy Spirit represented by the water of the membranes) that all of this will be accomplished. We are about to experience a new birth. It will challenge us and mess with our preconceived ideas, doctrines and theology, but it will not deviate from the Word of God. And if we are steadfast it will move us into a higher level."

Wrapping it Up:

That interpretation is only something that you can receive from the Spirit of God. That is not an interpretation that I can say, "She got it like this 'A-B-C". I know that Sarah received that revelation by the Spirit, and that is how you will receive the interpretation and revelation for any vision that you have.

The Scroll of Ezekiel

I have taken examples from the Word for the last two examples that I have used, because I felt that even though the others were visions that we have today, we needed to look to the Word as well. You need to see for yourself that this is not just something that happened to come upon us in the New Testament. Visions are something that have been with us throughout time. They have been with us right from Genesis.

The Vision:

I found a lovely example in Ezekiel 3:1-3

> *"Moreover He said to me, "Son of man, eat what you find; eat this scroll, and go, speak to the house of Israel."*
>
> *So I opened my mouth, and He caused me to eat that scroll.*
>
> *And He said to me, "Son of man, feed your belly, and fill your stomach with this scroll that I give you." So I ate, and it was in my mouth like honey in sweetness."*

Breakdown of the Vision:

Ezekiel was in prayer. He had just seen the Lord and the Lord gave a scroll to him and said, "Eat this scroll, Ezekiel." When did he have this vision? He had it while he was speaking to the Lord. This is an internal revelation. The revelation that Ezekiel received from the Lord was particularly for himself. The objects and symbols were for himself.

Interpretation:

> **VISION TYPE:** Internal
>
> **SPIRIT:** Positive
>
> **OBJECTS:** Scroll
>
> **ACTION:** Eating

INTERPRETATION: What was the spirit? It was obviously positive. The Lord was giving him things. What was the object? The object was the scroll, which speaks of the Word of the Lord. It always speaks of that in Scripture. The scroll represents God's Word. What did he do? He ate the scroll.

Can you see the symbolism? He took God's Word and he fed it into himself. And as he fed it into himself, you will read later on in Ezekiel how he stood up and spoke on the Lord's behalf. And all those words that he fed in now poured out, and he spoke in decree and proclamation, and he spoke as a prophet of God. The scroll, speaking of the Word and feeding it in, he took from the Lord the

Word, and the Lord placed His anointing within Ezekiel. That is what it represented. The Lord put His Words inside Ezekiel's spirit as he ate it in the spiritual realm. Then when it came time for him to speak, those words that he had taken in came out again and he spoke them with power.

Degradation of Israel

This is an example of a vision of proclamation from Ezekiel 40:3-4

> *"He took me there, and behold, there was a man whose appearance was like the appearance of bronze. He had a line of flax and a measuring rod in his hand, and he stood in the gateway.*
>
> *And the man said to me, "Son of man, look with your eyes and hear with your ears, and fix your mind on everything I show you; for you were brought here so that I might show them to you. Declare to the house of Israel everything you see."*

Breakdown of the Vision:

Can you see the difference in this vision? This is not a vision that was not for Ezekiel. The man who was standing there that looked like brass was an angel, and the angel was saying, "Okay, I'm about to show you a few things, Ezekiel, and when you see them I want you to use those visions that you see as a proclamation to speak forth."

This is really how the prophets of old operated. The Lord would show it to them in vision, and then they would declare it and speak it into the earth. By doing that they brought God's will to bear on the creation so that those events would come to pass.

Interpretation:

> **VISION TYPE:** External
>
> **SPIRIT:** Negative
>
> **CHARACTERS:** Sins of the people.
>
> **OBJECTS:** Idols and harlotry.
>
> **ACTION:** Ezekiel is called to proclaim.

INTERPRETATION: If you read the whole of Ezekiel you will see how the Lord took Ezekiel to different parts of Jerusalem, to the temple where they were worshipping idols, and the Lord showed Ezekiel each place where the Israelites had degraded themselves. They had totally turned against the Lord. As Ezekiel saw these visions, the Lord then took him and showed him a future vision of what was to become of Jerusalem and of the Israelites, and he spoke what was to come.

Unfortunately it was not such a positive word, but there were some positive things in there and the Lord gave

Ezekiel a pattern for the tabernacle. But can you see how he took those visions and he used them. He used the interpretation, he spoke them forth, he proclaimed them. He did not just keep them for his own interest. That is what we must do in our interpretations. Use them.

Apply the Interpretation

Who is like a wise man? And who knows the interpretation of a thing? A man's wisdom makes his face shine, and the sternness of his face is changed.

~ Ecclesiastes 8:1

Chapter 23 – Apply the Interpretation

Having dealt with the visions I come to my final point, which is applying the interpretation. It is no use getting a revelation for somebody in ministry if you do not follow through with that revelation and break them to freedom. If I had simply kept to myself the revelation that I had received of that little boy sitting in the corner, he would never ever have broken through to the victory that he did.

It was not enough for me just to see the vision. I had to apply the interpretation and I had to speak the Word of God into his life. I had to speak healing into that little boy's life and those hurts that had occurred. As I applied the interpretation he was set free instantly.

The same goes for the revelation that the Lord showed me for the stony heart. It was not enough for me simply to see the vision. I had to submit myself to His will. So as I submitted myself, His anointing came upon me and it shattered that stone. If I had just seen it and not taken it any further I would not have been set free. I would not be writing this book today, and I would not be ministering.

Do you see how vital it is to take the interpretation and follow it through to the end? The Lord is showing you a revelation for a reason. He is not just showing it so that you can know for interest sake. He is showing it to you so that you can minister to that person, so that you can see what their need is and reach in there and help them. You can see what is up ahead in their path and warn them, and then help them to overcome that.

That is really what it is all about - to know and then to move in there with faith, hope and love, help them overcome and help them to reach victory. That is just the best fruit that you can ever see in the life of somebody else. It is not so that you can look good, but to see that person break free from that bondage that you saw them in; to see that person blossom because of the revelation you shared. To not just give them revelation from your head, but to apply a force from the Spirit that brings the will of the Lord into being in their lives.

That is what it is about, to set people free, to heal broken hearts. Not to just get revelation, but to apply that revelation practically. As you do that you are going to start seeing the Body of Christ rising up piece by piece. As you are pouring into your brother and sister and bringing about that healing, and setting them free of that bondage by the revelation you have received, slowly the Body of Christ is going to start coming together. Instead of being dismembered and everybody running off and doing their own thing, we will be pouring into one another and we will come to stand as one.

Test the Spirits

Finally, test the spirits of your revelation. Make sure that you are speaking with the heart of faith, hope and love. We have shared in deception how any word that is forceful or brings guilt, fear or condemnation is not of the Spirit of the Lord. And when somebody is giving you an interpretation, test the spirits by the gift of discerning of spirits. And if you do not have that gift of discerning of spirits, Paul says that you are to desire such gifts.

If you would desire such a gift the Lord will grant it to you, and you would be able to reach out and claim that gift. If there is one gift that I have imparted to others the most, it has to be the gift of discerning of spirits, because it is vital in this day and age with the false prophets and false apostles rising up with the good and the bad. You need to test the spirits.

I do not like to put a damper on revelation, because visions are such a good and powerful force. But unfortunately there are those out there who would use it as a whip and would use it negatively to break down the Body of Christ instead of to build it up. There are those who would use it for their own means as part of the New Age heresy. They would use it for their own exhortation and to exalt themselves above the Lord Jesus. You need the gift of discerning of spirits. You need to know what is of God and you need to know what is not. When you know the difference it will set you free, because then you will be able to choose for yourself. Not only that, you will be able to feel the heart of God and minister that heart to somebody else, because you will discern the Spirit of God.

You see, to test the spirits does not just mean to discern evil, but it means to discern and feel the anointing as well. So when you are flowing in this gift, not only will you be able to watch out for the works of the enemy, but you will be able to sense the anointing of the Holy Spirit. So when you share, that anointing will be in your words and will go into the life of the person who is receiving from you. Also, when you receive, if you know how to test the spirits you will know what is of God. You will sense the Spirit of God on what the person is sharing.

Even better, with the gift of discerning of spirits you will be able to discern the condition of the spirit of somebody else. So when you come to minister to somebody you will able to know what is going on inside their spirit; if they are under bondage or even if they are blessed and anointed. You will be able to know, "Can I open my heart up to this person? Will I receive the anointing or will I receive a curse?"

Every member of the Body of Christ should be functioning in the gift of discerning of spirits. If we did we would identify each other by the Spirit of Christ that is within us instead of falling for the flakes and those wolves in sheep clothing who would seek to destroy you. It would cause unity to come in the Body of Christ.

Ultimate Goal

In conclusion, I would like to end off with a passage that is our ultimate goal. Numbers 12:6-8 says:

> *"Then He said, "Hear now My words: If there is a prophet among you, I, the Lord, make Myself known to him in a vision; I speak to him in a dream.*
>
> *Not so with My servant Moses; He is faithful in all My house.*
>
> *I speak with him face to face, even plainly, and not in dark sayings; and he sees the form of the Lord. Why then were you not afraid to speak against My servant Moses?"*

When you come to the place where it is no longer dark sayings in dreams and visions, but you are speaking with the Lord on a one-on-one basis, there is nothing that can stand against you in this world. Because as the Lord vindicated and stood up for Moses, so He will stand and vindicate you in your life. Everywhere you walk you will be a blessing. Every place you put your feet will be yours, according to the Word of God, because you will be speaking with the Lord mouth to mouth and face to face.

You will have a confidence that you have never had in your life before. You will stand in His authority. You will stand in His power, and you will stand in His Word. As you do that there is nothing that will not bow down before you. There is no sickness that will stand before

you. There is no poverty that will stand before you.
There is no demon that will stand before you. For just as
the Lord caused Korah to be swallowed up because of
his rebellion against Moses, so those who stand against
you will be swallowed up, and so those demons that
would dare defy you will be swallowed up by the power
of God.

That is what you should be aiming for. And do not think
that this is something that is for those who have been in
ministry for years and years. No! This is something that
every believer should be walking in. This is something
that you should be walking in, to know and hear the
voice of the Lord your God, to know and stand in His
assurance and to stand in His shadow. And to know that
as you stand in His shadow He fights on your behalf and
He speaks through you and uses you as a vessel mightily
for His use.

Impartation

I have imparted to you a lot of what has been in my
spirit in this chapter. I have poured out what has been in
my well, and I pray that as you have received it that it
would begin to churn and be stirred up in yours. I am
going to pray now and I am going to impart the gift of
discerning of spirits to you. I am going to impart to you
the ability to receive revelation for yourself, and not just
to receive that revelation, but to interpret it according to
faith, hope and love and by the Word of God.

If you are open to receive and if you truly desire this gift, there is nothing that will withhold this gift from you. I want you to open your heart and receive. I want you to reach out to the Lord right now and say, "Lord Jesus, I want this. I desire this. I want the gift of discerning of spirits. I want the ability and the spirit of wisdom and revelation. I want it now, Lord." Reach out now and claim it, because it is yours!

"Father I just pray that You would move on Your people right now in the name of Jesus. Come Holy Spirit and give them that spirit of wisdom and revelation. I impart right now the gift of discerning of spirits, that you would receive and know and discern. May you know that which is of the Lord! May you know which is the work of the enemy. May you be able to discern the spirit of your brother and your sister. May you come into their presence and may you know what is going on deep inside the recesses of their spirit, that you might reach in and that you might bring healing and change to their lives. May you know when the power of God is present in the life of another! May you know when a curse and the work of the enemy is present in the life of another.

When you receive a letter, when you watch a movie, when you watch a video or put on a tape, may you sense the spirit so strongly right within you that it shakes you to the core. When there is a spirit of evil on anything you pick up, anything you watch, anything you look at, anything you come into contact with, may your flesh react violently against it in Jesus' name! May you know! May it shake you, may it change you. May you know that this thing that you are touching is not of the Spirit of God and may you drop it and run! May you know which apostles are false. May you know which prophets are speaking out of their own desires instead of the desires of God. May your hair stand up on end. May you be shaken. May you have a knot in your stomach.

When the Spirit of God comes upon you, may you know that He has come upon you. When you pick up a book or a letter, when you read an email, may you know that the Spirit of God is upon it! May you feel the anointing from your head right down to your toes! May you be shaken. May you speak His Words. May you stand in His authority and in His power and may your life be changed!

I take off the blindfolds in the name of Jesus. Satan, you have blinded God's people for long enough and I stand against you in the Spirit of the Most High God and you will remove your hands off the eyes of God's people! For they will see, they will hear, they will know, and they will see your devices for once and for all. You will not trick them any longer, because the Body of Christ is rising up and you will not stand before it, Satan.

They are seeing and they are hearing and they are knowing and they will stand upon your head and they will crush you in the name of Jesus. The Body of Christ will be fooled and tricked no longer! The Word of God says that even the most elect will not be deceived; that many will be deceived, but the elect will not be deceived! The Body of Christ is the elect in this earth and they will not be deceived in the name of Jesus.

I speak that upon you right now in the name of Jesus. Your life will be changed, and it will be changed forever. You receive it, you claim it, you know it, because it is your gift and it is your right! It is God's desire for you right now.

Thank you Holy Spirit for making this come to pass in the lives of every single person who comes into contact with this. Shake and change Your Body. Open her eyes and let her stand on her feet in the power and authority that you have ordained her to stand in! In Jesus' name. Amen"

About the Author

Colette Toach
APOSTOLIC MOVEMENT INTERNATIONAL

Born in Bulawayo, Zimbabwe and raised in South Africa, Colette had a zeal to serve the Lord from a young age. Coming from a long line of Christian leaders and having grown up as a pastor's kid, she is no stranger to the realities of ministry. Despite having to endure many hardships such as her parent's divorce, rejection, and poverty, she continues to follow after the Lord passionately. Overcoming these obstacles early in her life has built a foundation of compassion and desire to help others gain victory in their lives.

Since then, the Lord has led Colette, with her husband, Craig Toach, to establish *Apostolic Movement International,* a ministry to train and minister to Christian leaders all over the world, where they share all the wisdom that the Lord has given them through each and every time they chose to walk through the refining fire in their personal lives, as well as in ministry.

In addition, Colette is a fantastic cook, an amazing mom to not only her 4 natural children, but to her numerous spiritual children all over the world. Colette is also a renowned author, mentor, trainer and a woman that has great taste in shoes! The scripture to "be all things to all men" definitely applies here, and the Lord keeps adding to that list of things each and every day.

How does she do it all? Experience through every book and teaching the life of an apostle firsthand, and get the insight into how the call of God can make every aspect of your life an incredible adventure.

Read more at www.colette-toach.com

Connect with Colette Toach on Facebook!
www.facebook.com/ColetteToach

Check Colette out on Amazon.com at:
www.amazon.com/author/colettetoach

Recommendations by the Author

Note: All reference of AMI refers to Apostolic Movement International.

Something you might not know is that this book and most of our other books are not just reading books, but are in fact text books. We and many other ministers use these textbooks in their church's and bible schools as courses across the world. These powerful resources have and are still changing lives and forging a standard in the body of Christ.

Schools of Apostolic Movement International (AMI):

Fivefold Ministry School: www.fivefold-school.com

Prophetic School: www.prophetic-school.com

Pastor Teacher School: www.pastorteacherschool.com

If you would like to use this book in your church or ministry, feel free to contact us directly for bulk offers and discounted prices to get you started.

See contact details at the end of the book.

Maybe *The Way of Dreams and Visions* gave you the answers you were looking for, but if you are one of those spiritually hungry pilgrims, then it is likely that I just whet your appetite and you are asking, "Ok, that was great, but what is for dessert?"

The Way of Dreams & Visions Symbol Dictionary

By Colette Toach

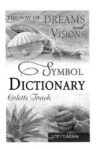

This is the symbols dictionary that replaces them all and the perfect companion to *The Way of Dreams and Visions*. Colette Toach does it again... she puts up a standard with an apostolic foundation that you can trust.

You will never have to look far and wide for an interpretation again.

There are many symbol dictionaries out there, but what stands out about ours is that each symbol is backed up by the Word and balanced by the Spirit. Combine the two together and you get a breeding ground for revelation.

Excerpt: The Way of Dreams & Visions Symbol Dictionary

Excerpt from: Naked – Nakedness

General Meaning

Nakedness in both dreams and visions speaks of being vulnerable and exposed.

Dreams

Positive

Perhaps you are someone that is not comfortable with opening up to others. If you dream of being naked and you do not care, it means that you are coming to the place where you are comfortable with being transparent with others.

So if you dream of walking around naked, but it does not bother you, it only means that you are being transparent and that you have nothing to hide. In ministry this is certainly a good thing.

Negative

If you are naked in your dream and you are uncomfortable with it, then it means that you feel exposed or vulnerable at the moment. You feel that you are overwhelmed and that you cannot handle the situation that you are in.

It can also mean that you are perhaps being TOO transparent with people that you should not be sharing absolutely everything with.

Although we need to be open to the Lord and our fellow believers, there are times when we need to keep things to ourselves so that the enemy does not get wind of what God is doing.

Visions

Positive

In my book, The Journey of Tamar, there is a chapter where she is stripped of all her old clothing so that she can be clothed again in something new. It was a picture of the process the Lord took me through and one many believers face.

As you have looked to the Lord for blessing or a new ministry, He is going to take you through change. It will mean letting go of the old and allowing Him to strip you first. Only then can He give you the new blessing that He has for you.

If you have desired to enter into a relationship with the Lord and you see yourself (or someone else) naked, the interpretation is clear.

The Lord is saying that before you can progress you need to allow yourself to be naked before Him. He already knows your sins and your failures, so you do not need to fear. However, unless you let down your guard and allow the Lord into those secret parts of your life, you will never progress.

You never need to feel afraid of being naked before the Lord, because He does not intend to leave you that way. He simply intends to heal your wounds and re-clothe you in royalty!

> *Genesis 2:25 And they were both **naked**, the man and his wife, and were not ashamed.*

Negative

Nakedness spoke of shame in Scripture, and this is certainly true when you have faced hurts in your life.

If you see yourself (or someone else in personal ministry) naked, dirty and bleeding, it is a picture of the hurts you have endured in the past and that still plague you today.

See also: Bathroom, Shower

Customer Review

Thank you Apostle Colette for the *Way of Dreams and Visions Symbol Dictionary* (Book). It has helped me tremendously. I am still working through some of the dreams and visions the Lord has given to me. It is so cool that God can speak to us through dreams and visions.

However, my communicating with him in this unique manner protects me from pursuing someone else's dreams and visions, their ideas, precepts and concepts.

This book is likened unto a candlelight that has helped me to organize my thoughts and God-given ideas. I have so much clarity, and my understanding is so much better now.

However, as I go through this book - I was very surprised to find that most of my dreams have already come to pass. This book can serve as a spiritual guide for anyone who is stuck in a rut and cannot get out! For those different ones out there - who are seeking direction in the area of dreams and visions - I recommend this book highly!

Practical Prophetic Ministry

By Colette Toach

Wouldn't it be incredible if someone could have walked you through your prophetic calling and pointed out all the potholes before you fell into them?

Unfolded step by step, you will have someone along the way telling you what to avoid, what to embrace and most importantly... what to do next along your prophetic journey.

Taking you through training and pointing out the way you need to go, it is a must if you have a prophetic calling.

Prophetic Essentials

Book 1 of the Prophetic Field Guide Series

By Colette Toach

In this book, you will find out that the call of the prophet goes far deeper than the functions and duties that the prophet fulfills. Anyone flowing in prophetic ministry can carry out tasks similar to the prophet.

If it burns in you to pay any price that is necessary and to stand up and break down the barriers between the Lord Jesus and His Bride, then my friend, you have picked up the right tool that will confirm the fire in your belly and the call of God on your life.

I'm Not Crazy - I'm a Prophet

By Colette Toach

It takes a prophet to know a prophet!

You do not have to follow in the footsteps of others before you take the wealth of this book and rise above the pit falls.

That is why Colette Toach can take the prophetic and dish it out in its truth and cover the subjects included in this book.

So are you Crazy? Maybe a little, but this book will help you to be the true prophet that God has called you to be!

The Journey of Tamar: An Allegory for the Prophet

By Colette Toach

'Ordinary' was never in Tamar's vocabulary. However, when the Mighty Eagle finds her, she is living a life that is stuck in a rut of reality. He called her on the adventure of a lifetime.

Join Tamar on a journey that will shape her from a child into the warrior she was always meant to be. Along the way, you might find out that it is you that has been called on the adventure of a lifetime.

How to Hear the Voice of God (Study Group Kit)

By Colette Toach

Knowing the Lord is more than just understanding the principles of the Word. It is learning to know when He is speaking and to share in the secrets in His heart.

By the time you are finished with this course, you will discover that God does not have favorites, but that every believer can hear from Him clearly.

A.M.I. Prophetic School

www.prophetic-school.com

 Whether you are just starting out or have been along the way for some time, we all have questions.

Who better to answer them than another prophet!

With over 18 years of experience, the A.M.I. Prophetic School is the leader in the prophetic realm.

From dedicated lecturers to live streaming and graduation, the A.M.I. Prophetic School is your home away from home.

What Our Prophetic Training Accomplishes

Our extensive training is a full two-year curriculum that will:

1. Identify and confirm your prophetic call
2. Effectively train you to flow in all the gifts of the Spirit
3. Fulfill your purpose as a prophet in the local church
4. Take your hand through the prophetic training process
5. Specialist training in spiritual warfare
6. Arm you for intercession and decree
7. Minister in praise and worship
8. Achieve prophetic maturity

Contact Information

To check out our wide selection of materials, go to:
www.ami-bookshop.com

Do you have any questions about any products?

Contact us at: +1 (760) 466 - 7679
(9am to 5pm California Time, Weekdays Only)

E-mail Address: admin@ami-bookshop.com

Postal Address:

> A.M.I
> 5663 Balboa Ave #416
> San Diego, CA 92111, USA

Facebook Page:
http://www.facebook.com/ApostolicMovementInternational

YouTube Page:
https://www.youtube.com/c/ApostolicMovementInternational

Twitter Page: https://twitter.com/apmoveint

Amazon.com Page: www.amazon.com/author/colettetoach

AMI Bookshop – It's not Just Knowledge, It's **Living Knowledge**

Made in the USA
San Bernardino, CA
07 February 2020

64178644R00191